CONTENTS

PREFACE   4

INTRODUCTION:
ROMAN BRITAIN AND HISTORY   5

1 THE PEOPLES OF BRITAIN   23

2 NATIVES AND THE ROMAN SYSTEM   45

3 ROMAN AUTHORITY AND ITS DEMANDS   68

4 ART: CELTIC TRADITIONS AND THEIR
   ROMANIZATION   85

5 THE GODS: RITUALS OF LIFE AND DEATH   100

6 THE END OF ROMAN RULE   130

   RETROSPECT   135

   PLACES TO VISIT   136

   FURTHER READING   137

   GLOSSARY   139

   INDEX   142

PREFACE

This book is not a conventional history of Roman Britain. It attempts to approach the subject in a new way, laying emphasis on the social, economic and cultural history that can be gleaned from diverse archaeological and historical sources. By concentrating on the archaeological evidence I have attempted to provide a balanced introduction and one that the general reader may find accessible. Equally I hope to have offered some new thoughts of interest to those who already have a good knowledge of Roman Britain.

This book took some time in gestation. It began life as a more extensive work commissioned by another publisher. I am most grateful to Stephen Johnson and Peter Kemmis Betty for taking it into this series. The first draft was largely written during a term's Research Leave held at Churchill College, Cambridge in 1991. I am grateful to the College, and especially Dick Whittaker and Henry Hurst for making that profitable and enjoyable stay possible. Equally I thank Durham University for their generous grant of Research Leave.

When the decision was made to produce a second edition of this book, I decided to update the text without major alteration. I have corrected several errors kindly pointed out by Richard Reece. The book still forms a useful general introduction to the subject. I have altered some sections to reflect the results of recent research, but I have not changed the format to take account of changes in the emphasis of research seen in the past decade. That would have involved writing an entirely different book. I have used the opportunity provided by being allowed further colour pictures to add some new material and to widen the scope of the illustrations.

A number of colleagues have kindly helped in various ways. I would particularly thank Simon James, Anne Marshall and Richard Reece for reading drafts and making comments on how to improve it. Also I have benefited from ideas stimulated by the works of many others too numerous to mention, but especially among the staff and students of the Department of Archaeology in Durham.

Fitzwilliam College, Cambridge
December 2004

ENGLISH HERITAGE

ROMAN BRITAIN

MARTIN MILLETT

B.T BATSFORD

ACKNOWLEDGEMENTS

IN MEMORY OF MY FATHER

First published 1995

This revised edition published 2005

© M. J. Millett 1995, 2005

The right of M. J. Millett to be identified as Author of this work has been asserted by him in accordance with the Copyright, Designs and Patents Act 1988.

Volume © B T Batsford Ltd

ISBN 0 7134 8951 0

A CIP catalogue record for this book is available from the British Library.

Printed in Singapore by Kyodo
for the publishers
B T Batsford
Chysalis Books Group
The Chrysalis Building
Bramley Road
London W10 6SP

www.chrysalisbooks.co.uk

A member of **Chrysalis** Books plc

Unless otherwise stated the drawings are by Yvonne Beadnell and photographs are from the Department of Archaeology, University of Durham. The sources of the other illustrations are as follows: P. Halkon (*11, 59*), RIB 288 from R.G. Collingwood and R.P. Wright *The Roman Inscriptions Britain, Vol. 1,* by kind permission of the Administrators of the Haverfield Bequest (*12*), Photographs © the Trustees of the British Museum (*13, 37, 72, 80, 82, 83, 92, 97*), Fitzwilliam Museum (*14*), Museum of London (*38, 39, 81, 91, 93, 105*), MOLAS (*15, 20, 103*), Courtesy of Simon James (*18*), Crown Copyright, NMR (*23, 48, 51*), English Heritage, NMR (*26, 27, 36, 57, 60, 64, 78, 104*), Barbara McNee (*22, 41, 44*), The Manchester Museum, the University of Manchester (*24*), Photograph by Leslie Still, courtesy of R. Daniels (*25*), Copyright Royal Commission on the Ancient and Historical Monuments of Scotland (*30*), K. McBarron, Dept of Archaeology, Durham University (*35*), Hull and East Riding Museum – Hull City Council Museums and Art Gallery, (*40*), Pre-Construct Archaeology Ltd, courtesy of F. Meddens (*45*), G.W.G. Allen, courtesy of the Ashmolean Museum, Oxford (*52*), Fishbourne Roman Palace/Sussex Archaeological Society (*53*), D.S. Neal, courtesy of the Society of Antiquaries of London (*55,*), author (*3, 19, 28, 61, 63, 67, 75, 76, 83*), Museum of Antiquities of the University and Society of Antiquaries of Newcastle upon Tyne, courtesy of Lindsay Allason-Jones (*66*), from A. Bulleid and H. St George Gray *The Glastonbury Lake Village Vol.1* (1911) (*69*), Wiltshire Heritage Museum, Devizes (*70*), Fishbourne Roman Palace (*73*), Institute of Archaeology, University of Oxford, courtesy of Professor B.W. Cunliffe (*75*), Tullie House Museum and Art Gallery, Carlisle (*77*), © the Trustees of the National Museums of Scotland (*86*), Institute of Archaeology, University of Oxford, courtesy of Professor B.W. Cunliffe and Roger Tomlin (who also kindly provided the amended reading of the text used in the caption) (*90*), J.H. Gillings, Surrey Heath Archaeological Trust (*94*), from *Archaeologia, 25* (1834) (*98*), from *Archaeologia, 26* (1836) (*99*), Brian Dix, Northamptonshire Archaeological Unit (*101*), Copyright Royal Archaeological Institute, from *The Archaeological Journal,* 140 (1983) (*102*), David S. Neal (photographs provided by the Royal Commission on the Historical Monuments of England) (*56, 78*), from Buckman and Newmarch *Illustrations of the Remains of Roman Art in Cirencester* (1850) (*79*), G. Huxley, Alton Excavation Committee (*98*).

INTRODUCTION: ROMAN BRITAIN AND HISTORY

Roman Britain has attracted much attention from historians and remains among the most fascinating periods in British history. For the first time, Britain moved on to the fringes of a society that has left written records. She also passed through a phase that has left rich archaeological monuments that can hardly fail to stir the imagination. Recent years have seen an awakening of interest in how indigenous British society responded to Roman control, developing a culture in which Classical and Celtic features merged. The period is one of unusual richness and rapid changes which helped to shape later centuries.

Britain's place in the Roman world was always marginal. Even Caesar's expeditions to Britain in 55 and again in 54 BC must be seen against the backdrop of the political situation at Rome where he was a central player in the internal conflicts of his time. He held control of a large army in Gaul and his campaigns were undertaken on the pretext of a military threat to Rome's territory. His expeditions to Britain were justified on the grounds that its people were aiding the Gauls, although we should not overlook the immense prestige that military success brought him. The timing of his successful crossings to Britain contributed to the retention of the military command which had been under threat of withdrawal and was due to lapse at the end of 54 BC. Continued military power was of vital importance to his survival and continuing political status. The material rewards to be obtained from Britain were negligible but the act of crossing the 'Ocean' had immense symbolic

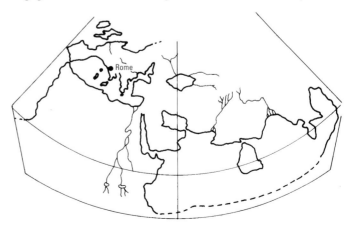

1 *(right)* Map based on the work of the second-century AD Greek geographer Ptolemy, showing Britain's place in the Roman world. Ancient geographers saw the world as surrounded by the 'Ocean' that flowed around it. Britain was right on the edge of the known world and so was a place of mystery.

2 *(above)* Reconstruction of the Arch of Claudius in Rome, which was built as part of one of the city's aqueducts. The arch was dedicated in AD 51 and celebrated Claudius' victory in Britain eight years earlier. A fragment of its main inscription is shown in (3).

significance as it was viewed as a river that defined the very edge of the world (1).

Caesar's *Commentaries* on his wars were propaganda written for people at Rome. Although Britain remained largely outside direct Roman control for nearly another century, Caesar's expeditions had brought her within the Roman sphere. Events at the centre of the empire meant that there was little serious interest in Britain until about AD 40 when the deranged Emperor Gaius (Caligula) took an army to the shore of the 'Ocean', but set it to gather shells rather than invade Britain! His successor, Claudius, did send an army of conquest in AD 43, although his motives remain uncertain. On his accession Claudius' main problem was his lack of military reputation, so his most likely intention in sending the army was to obtain a rapid and spectacular victory (2). His repetition of Caesar's glorious crossing of the Ocean will not have been lost on contemporaries (3).

Once annexed, Britain long remained a place of military activity, and such events attracted most attention from Roman writers. Britain remained remote from political events at Rome and had no reputation as a source of wealth. It is very doubtful that wealth was expected to accrue from her conquest, at least after the initial spoils of war had been claimed by the invading army. The empire's provinces were an accidental by-product of politically motivated conquest and were rarely viewed as an economic resource to be exploited systematically.

Full conquest was never achieved, although under the Governor Agricola (AD 77–83) (see 6) and again under the Emperor Severus (AD 208–11) (see 9) campaigns reached far into Scotland. Britain's

3 *(right)* Photograph of the surviving fragments of the principal inscription from the Arch of Claudius. In translation the whole of the inscription would have read: 'The Senate and People of Rome dedicated this to Tiberius Claudius Caesar Augustus Germanicus (son of Drusus, chief priest, during his eleventh tenure of tribunician powers, consul five times, hailed as commander-in-chief twenty-two times, censor, father of his country) because he received into surrender eleven kings of the Britons conquered without loss and he first brought the barbarian peoples across the Ocean under the authority of the Roman people.'

position and relative insignificance left her on the edge of Rome's sphere of interest; as the empire collapsed in on itself Britain became increasingly marginal. In the relative peace which prevailed, the populace developed a Romanized culture of their own which survived well into the fourth century. Only early in the fifth century when military problems at the centre of the empire coincided with those in Britain was a choice forced and Britain divorced from the Roman world. Standard histories of Roman Britain frequently focus on an account of the conquest and development of the province from its first contacts with Rome to the withdrawal of the last troops in the early fifth century. Most rely heavily on Classical authors whose accounts concern Rome's strivings to conquer and subdue the native inhabitants by military means and through the imposition of alien administrative and social systems. The weakness of that approach lies in its emphasis on things Roman because the native inhabitants left no written accounts of their own, and were less materially rich and so archaeologically more elusive. As a result, discussions of the native peoples have tended to concentrate on what was Roman about them rather than what was British.

THE EVIDENCE FOR ROMAN BRITAIN

The contents of the historical texts that concern Roman Britain are summarized in the following table, which is accompanied by maps showing the progress of Roman annexation.

Dates	Events	Sources
55–54 BC	Julius Caesar, engaged on his conquest of Gaul, made two military expeditions to Britain. The first in 55 BC was of limited success although it generated a useful propaganda advantage in Rome where Britain was known as a mysterious place on the other side of the 'Ocean'. The larger-scale campaign in 54 BC was more successful and resulted in the imposition of a treaty on the tribes of the southeast, which marks the first stage of a projected Roman annexation.	Caesar, *Gallic Wars*, V
54 BC–AD 43	Events, first in Gaul then at Rome, prevented any capitalization on Caesar's success. Diplomatic contacts between British tribes and Rome continued with the arrival in Rome of tribal leaders deposed in Britain under Augustus (27 BC–AD 14) and Caligula (AD 37–41). Both Augustus and Caligula (in AD 40) are said to have considered invading Britain, although neither acted.	*Res Gestae*, 32 Tacitus, *Annals*, II Dio Cassius, LIII Tacitus, *Annals*, II
54 BC–AD 43	There was also commercial contact, with the export of products from Britain and imports from the empire, which seems to have been worthwhile for Rome.	Strabo, IV

Rome influenced political evolution in Britain and this engendered conflict between the tribes. Although outside the territory of the empire, some of the tribes remained as clients of successive emperors and had close contacts with Rome. This was a period of rapid development and the growth of one dominant native tribe, the Catuvellauni, whose capital lay at Camulodunon (Colchester). Their expansion squeezed the adjacent tribes, and deposed leaders appealed to Rome to help re-establish themselves.

Dates	Events	Sources
AD 43	The last such leader was Berikos (Verica) who fled to the Emperor Claudius leading the latter to intervene. Claudius, anxious to obtain prestige through military success, sent an invasion force of about 40,000 men (**4**). The force moved through southern England, and took the principal native centre, Camulodunon (Colchester), under Claudius' personal command. Claudius accepted the surrender of eleven British kings, and was honoured at Rome where he returned immediately.	Dio Cassius, LX Suetonius, *Claudius*, 17 Inscription, CIL V no. 920 (see **3**) Dio Cassius, LX
AD 43–60	Following the defeat of the southeastern tribes, campaigning continued in the southwest under the command of the future emperor Vespasian, who won a series of victories. A revolt occurred in East Anglia (in AD 47), but the expansion of the Roman occupation continued into Wales where it was slowed by the guerrilla tactics of the natives, and by a revolt in the Pennines. Early in the reign of Nero (AD 54–68) consideration was given to withdrawal, presumably because of slow military progress.	Suetonius, *Vespasian*, 4 Tacitus, *Annals*, XII Suetonius, *Nero*, 18
AD 58–60	Campaigns were undertaken against the Druids on Anglesey.	Tacitus, *Annals*, XIV
AD 60	East Anglia rose against the Romans under the leadership of Queen Boudicca, with the destruction of the Roman towns of Colchester, London and Verulamium.	Tacitus, *Annals*, XIV
AD 61–71	The crushing of the revolt was followed by a period of consolidation (**5**).	Tacitus, *Agricola*, XVI
AD 71–4	The allied kingdom of the Brigantes in the Pennines was riven with internal strife, so Rome intervened and conquered the area.	Tacitus, *Histories*, III, 45 & *Agricola*, XVII
AD 74–7	Expansion of the Roman province continued with the subjugation of south Wales.	Tacitus, *Agricola*, XVII
AD 77–83 AD 80	The new governor, Agricola, led a sustained series of campaigns that enlarged the province substantially. First he completed the conquest of Wales and Anglesey, then he turned to the consolidation of northern Britain, before moving into Scotland where he reached the Tay in AD 80. He garrisoned the area up to the Forth-Clyde isthmus, and dealt with southwest Scotland, at the same time suggesting to Rome that Ireland would be easy to conquer (**6**).	Tacitus, *Agricola*, XVIII–XXXVIII

Dates	Events	Sources
AD 82	Agricola again advanced northwards up the eastern coastal plain, leading to the establishment of a garrison as far as the Tay.	
AD 83	The great set-piece battle of Mons Graupius, somewhere in northeast Scotland, marked the successful completion of Agricola's campaigns (**6**). At this stage Britain was also circumnavigated by Agricola's fleet.	
c. AD 87	Following Agricola's departure, Roman military attention was turned to the Danube, and as a result troops from Britain were removed, with resultant withdrawal from Scotland.	Inscription, ILS no. 2719

The historical sources for the next thirty years are very poor but it is suggested, on the basis of the distribution of forts and dated pottery, that the army was slowly withdrawn from most of Scotland and the occupied zone contracted to the area based on a line from the Tyne to the Solway.

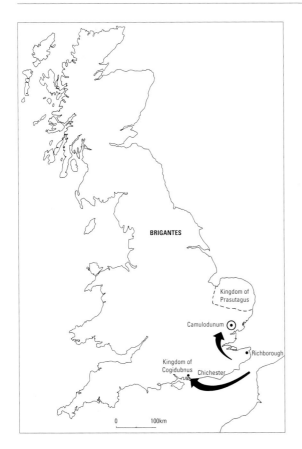

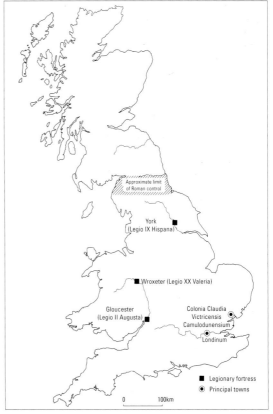

4 *(above)* Map showing the progress of the Claudian invasion of Britain. Richborough appears to have been the principal landing base although some suggest that the landing took place near Chichester in the Kingdom of Cogidubnus. Camulodunon, later called Camulodunum (Colchester), was the main target for the first campaign.

5 *(above)* Map showing the progress of the annexation of Britain to the early 70s AD. After the initial stages of annexation, the main army bases were established in the north and west overlooking territory still to be conquered, while towns were established in the southeast.

Dates	Events	Sources
AD 122	Hadrian visited Britain following a military disturbance. The construction of Hadrian's Wall, built 'to separate the Romans from the barbarians', followed shortly afterwards (**7**).	*Scriptores Historiae Augustae* (SHA), *Hadrian*, 5; 11
AD 139–42	The new emperor, Antoninus Pius, abandoned Hadrian's Wall and advanced northwards, driving back the barbarians, before constructing a new wall between the Forth and the Clyde (**8**).	SHA, *Antoninus Pius*, 5
AD 138–61	Antoninus Pius may have removed territory from the Brigantes and fought a war in the Genounian region although this reference may not concern Britain at all.	Pausanius, *Description of Greece*, VIII, 43

The evidence for the following period is ephemeral and ambiguous. The conventional interpretation that the Antonine Wall was abandoned in the mid-150s and then briefly reoccupied again until 163–4 has recently been revised. It is now thought that the withdrawal back to Hadrian's Wall was piecemeal and took place through the period between 155 and 163–4.

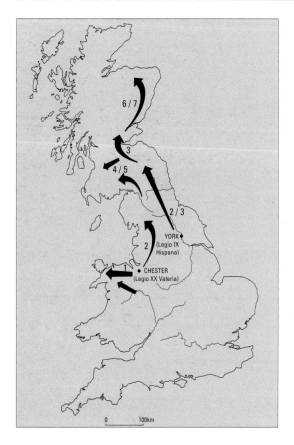

6 *(above)* **Map showing Agricola's campaigns in Britain (AD 77–83). The numerals indicate the numbering of the successive years of campaigning according to his son-in-law Tacitus' biography.**

7 *(above)* **Map showing the military dispositions in Britain towards the end of Hadrian's reign (AD 117–36). This marks the culmination of the process of retrenchment after the withdrawal from Scotland in the latter part of the first century.**

Dates	Events	Sources
AD 181–4	Tribes invaded across Hadrian's Wall, but were repulsed.	Dio Cassius, LXXII
AD 184–5	Emperor Commodus took the title Britannicus, issuing coins to commemorate victory in Britain.	Coins, RIC 437, 440, 451
AD 185	A mutiny among the troops in Britain led to the downfall of Perennis, the praetorian prefect in Rome. As a result, Commodus appointed the future emperor Pertinax as Governor of Britain.	Dio Cassius, LXXII SHA, *Pertinax, 3*
AD 192 AD 193 AD 193–6 AD 196–7	Commodus and then his successor Pertinax were assassinated, and in the struggle for the succession Clodius Albinus, the governor of Britain, was one of three contenders. For an initial period, Septimius Severus recognized him as his deputy (i.e. Caesar) while fighting against the third pretender, Pescennius Niger. Once he was defeated, Severus and Albinus engaged in a civil war, with Albinus taking troops from Britain with him. Severus won after a major battle outside Lyon. Following his victory Severus divided Britain into two provinces, probably to ensure that no single governor again had command of so large an army.	Dio Cassius, LXXIII Dio Cassius, LXXIII Herodian, II, 15 Dio Cassius, LXXV Herodian, III, 8

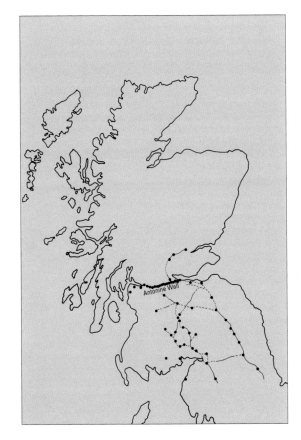

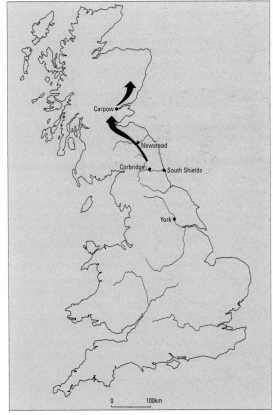

8 *(above)* Map showing the new northern frontier zone created after Antoninus Pius reoccupied southern Scotland in AD 139–45. This new frontier did not last long and before the end of the century Hadrian's Wall was again the northern limit of Roman control.

9 *(above)* Map showing the campaigns of Septimius Severus in Scotland during the period AD 208–11.

Dates	Events	Sources
AD 197–205	The tribes of the Maeatae and Caledonians in Scotland broke their treaty with Rome and waged war in the north. Since Roman military concerns lay elsewhere, the Maeatae were bought off.	Dio Cassius, LXXV
AD 208–11	Renewed troubles in Britain provided the opportunity for the emperor (Severus) to come in person with his sons to campaign in Scotland. He defeated the Caledonians but this was followed by a revolt of the Maeatae, and a renewed guerrilla war by the Caledonians. While preparing for the campaign of 211 Severus died in York. He was succeeded by his sons, Geta and Caracalla, who terminated the expedition and withdrew from the territory gained (**9**).	Dio Cassius, LXXVI Herodian, III, 14–15 Dio Cassius, LXXVII; Herodian, III, 15

After 244 the structure of authority within the empire failed, and there was a period of about 40 years during which emperors neither maintained power for long, nor ensured a peaceful succession. In the period from 259 to 274 Britain formed part of the Gallic empire, which had effectively seceded from the remainder of the empire. Political stability was restored with the accession of Aurelian (270–5) and consolidated by Diocletian (from 284), who shared power with Maximian from 286. Within Britain the events of the mid-third century up to this period are little known.

Dates	Events	Sources
AD 286–9	Carausius was appointed to police the English Channel, which was infested with barbarians. His success enabled him to profit from booty, and for exploiting this he was sentenced to death by the emperor. He responded by declaring himself emperor. His control of Britain was unchallenged until Maximian launched a naval attack, which seems to have been repulsed. Carausius then occupied parts of northern Gaul.	Aurelius Victor, 39; Eutropius, IX. 21 Panegyric on Maximian, 11–12
AD 293	Constantius, Maximian's deputy (i.e. Caesar), attacked and took Boulogne. Carausius was assassinated by one of his ministers, Allectus, who was declared emperor in Britain and northern Gaul.	Panegyric on Constantius Caesar, 6 Eutropius, IX, 22
AD 296	Constantius' army attacked, landing on the south coast, and Allectus was killed. Constantius was accorded a triumphal welcome in London.	Panegyric on Constantius Caesar, 13–20
AD 305–6	Constantius, now co-emperor with Maximian, came to northern Britain to conduct a military campaign. He was joined by his son Constantine, and reached the far north of Scotland. While staying at York the emperor died, and Constantine was declared emperor.	Aurelius Victor, 40; Eutropius, X,1–2
AD 312–14	Coins show that the Emperor Constantine was in Britain. In 315 he took the title Britannicus indicating that he had won a victory here.	Coins, RIC 133–41, 142–3, 144–5
AD 342–3	A winter visit to Britain by the Emperor Constans suggests a crisis here.	Libianus, *Orationes,* LIX
AD 350–3	A revolt in Gaul toppled Constans, who was replaced by Magnentius. The defeat of the rebellion was followed by major reprisals in Britain.	Ammianus Marcellinus, XIV, 5
AD 360	Troops were sent to Britain to deal with the Picts and Scots (although the motive may have been simply to remove the troops from Gaul).	Ammianus Marcellinus, XX, 1
AD 364	Barbarian raids by Picts, Scots and Saxons are recorded.	Ammianus Marcellinus, XXVI, 4
AD 367–8	A concerted barbarian attack occurred, with the loss of a senior military commander. Count Theodosius was sent to recover the situation and we are told that he restored the province after a major campaign.	Ammianus Marcellinus, XXVII, 8; XXVIII, 3

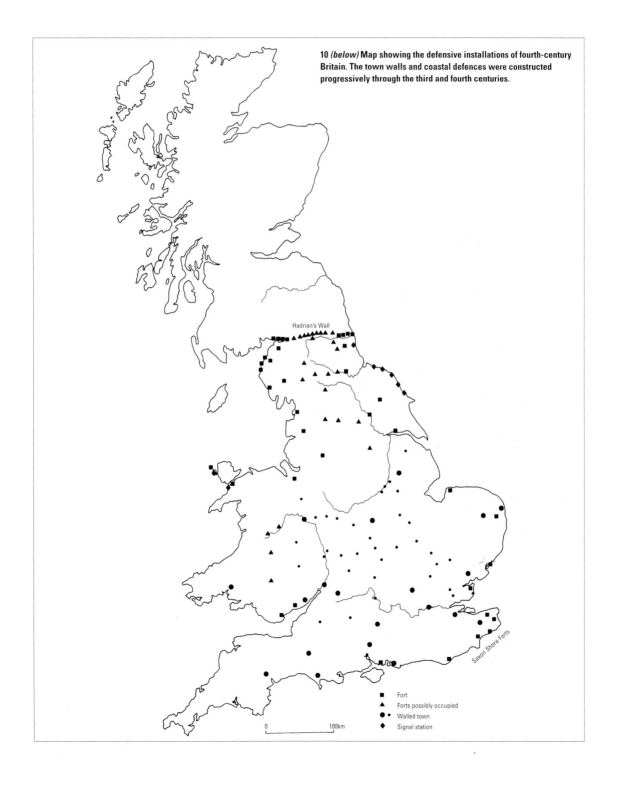

10 *(below)* Map showing the defensive installations of fourth-century Britain. The town walls and coastal defences were constructed progressively through the third and fourth centuries.

Hadrian's Wall

Saxon Shore Forts

■ Fort
▲ Forts possibly occupied
● Walled town
◆ Signal station

0   100km

Dates	Events	Sources
AD 383–8	Magnus Maximus, a British army commander, headed another revolt, killing the Emperor Gratian. Maximus gained control of much of the western empire and ruled it from Trier. He moved against Italy and was defeated by Theodosius.	Zosimus, IV, 35; 37 Orosius, VII, 35
AD 396–8	The general Stilicho ordered an expedition against the barbarians in Britain.	Claudian, *Stilicho,* II, 247–55
AD 399	Peace was restored by Stilicho's expedition.	Claudian, *Eutropius*, I, 391–3
AD 401–2	Troops were withdrawn by Stilicho to defend Italy.	Claudian, *Gothic War,* 416–18
AD 406–7	A usurper, Marcus, took power in Britain. Marcus was replaced first by Gratian then by Constantine III. Constantine was left to defend Gaul against the barbarians.	Zosimus, VI, 2 Orosius, VII, 40
AD 408–9	Britain is attacked by the Saxons. 'The Britons freed themselves, expelling their Roman governors and setting up their own administration.'	Zosimus, VI, 5
AD 410	The Emperor Honorius replied to an appeal for help from Britain by telling the cities to look after their own defence.	Zosimus, VI, 10
AD 429	St Germanus visited Britain to counter heresy in the church and defeated a Saxon raiding party.	Constantius, *Vita*
AD 435–7	St Germanus may have visited Britain for a second time.	Constantius, *Vita*

The accounts of events after the first decade of the fifth century are difficult to interpret. There were clearly continuing Saxon raids, which resulted in the loss of territory. By this stage events at Rome prevented any help being sent from outside Britain. It is likely that from shortly after 400 the government of the province had degenerated, with effective power moving into the hands of the landed aristocracy who acted as local barons. From the 440s land was lost to the Saxons piecemeal, as a result of the limited power of the local lords. Territory in Kent seems to have been lost first, but there remained a strong sub-Roman enclave in the west and north, which certainly lasted down to the early sixth century. It is to this period that the legendary King Arthur belongs as a symbol of sub-Roman power against the Saxons.

Writing an historical account based on these written sources poses two challenges. First, there is only limited evidence. Second, as all the sources were written by and for the elite who controlled the empire, they are almost exclusively Mediterranean in outlook. They were written not to provide an unbiased account of their world for posterity, but to influence and impress contemporaries within their own highly competitive social and political milieu. They have comparatively little to tell us about affairs and life within Britain except where pertinent to events and attitudes at Rome; hence the themes of wars and conquest upon which political success at Rome was founded. This propagandist character frequently results in exaggeration and selective reporting which is difficult to evaluate in the absence of alternative contemporary views.

11 *(above)* Aerial photograph of the Iron Age and Roman landscape near Holme, on Spalding Moor in East Yorkshire. Differential crop growth, emphasized by shadow in low-angled sunlight, reveals the buried ditches of settlement enclosures and field systems showing something of the layout of the countryside.

The vital political nature of many of them is also illustrated by the laudatory character of texts written in praise of particular individuals. Such active writing and rewriting of history was common, and may be illustrated by the account that the late Roman historian Ammianus Marcellinus gave of the defeat of a barbarian attack on Britain in AD 367–8. This casts the general, Count Theodosius, as a hero who 'restored Britain' after defeating the invaders. This is often accepted as reliable, without sufficient note being taken of the circumstances in which Ammianus was writing: he lived at the court of the Emperor Theodosius I, son of the general concerned.

Where texts do concern the details of events, they are often geographically unspecific as it was the military success that was important, not its location within a country which was largely unknown to the intended readership. For instance, the precise location of the decisive battle at Mons Graupius that marked the culmination of Agricola's campaigns in Scotland in AD 83 remains unknown, and probably unknowable, despite the central place of this Roman victory in Tacitus' account of his father-in-law's life.

The written sources are also geographically limited as the Roman occupation was largely confined to the mainland, south of the Tyne. Campaigns did take place in Scotland, and Ireland, too, was known through diplomatic and trading contacts, but it seems there was insufficient knowledge of either area to generate any substantial literature.

Where references are made to regions beyond the frontiers or to tribal groups before their incorporation by Rome, it is not always clear how far they contain information of substance rather than rhetorical descriptions of familiar stereotyped images of savages. Caesar's celebrated and much-quoted description of the peoples of Britain at the time of his expeditions in 55 and 54 BC tells us that those living away from the coast did not grow corn, but lived on milk, clothed themselves in animal skins and painted their bodies blue. This lively image, popularly illustrated in schoolbooks, gives a fascinating insight into the Roman stereotype of a barbarian but is almost wholly contradicted by the archaeological evidence we have of peoples who inhabited Britain in the first century BC.

In addition to these literary works, several bureaucratic documents have survived through accidents of history. These include the *Antonine Itinerary* (a list of stopping-places on routes through the empire), Ptolemy's *Geography* of the second century, and the *Notitia Dignitatum* of the fifth century, which lists the insignia and dignitaries of the empire, perhaps derived from files compiled down to about AD 408. Despite problems with their interpretation, these texts, together with inscriptions, enable us to identify the names of settlements and the tribes of Roman Britain.

Given the character of the texts, any modern account based solely on written evidence will almost inevitably be restricted by the direction of the original narrative and the nature of the views presented. Using such an account is like trying to explore a tract of countryside without ever leaving the road. While it is vital to take account of the contents of the literary sources, it is inappropriate to define the structure of this book around them. My intention is, therefore, to produce a narrative that does not simply supplement written sources with other information but rather places the Classical texts within a framework defined by the archaeological evidence. In order to achieve this end it is important first to understand the nature of the archaeological evidence.

THE CHARACTER OF ARCHAEOLOGICAL EVIDENCE

Archaeological remains are the physical survivals of the past in the present. They include the structures of buildings and settlements, and the objects used by their inhabitants. The archaeological record was not created with the same conscious and contemporary biases as the historical texts, but is no less challenging to interpret; much of it is the accidental by-product of past activity which provides clues about the behaviour of those who created it. However, two sets of problems must be borne in mind when it is used: first, there are differences in how various materials have survived; second, we have to discover how to read the evidence.

Archaeological materials vary in nature and importance in different regions and through time. From the Roman period the basic evidence consists of sites with their associated landscape features and objects (**12**). Sites differ in size and character ranging from the small farmsteads of less than 10,000 square metres (a hectare) to the largest of the towns, London, whose defended area alone covered 1.335 sq km (133.5 ha). They had an array of forms,

12 *(above)* Monumental inscription from the forum at Wroxeter, commemorating the construction of the building in AD 129–30. In translation it reads: 'For the Emperor Caesar Trajan Hadrian Augustus (son of the deified Trajan, conqueror of Parthia, grandson of the deified Nerva), chief priest, in the fourteenth year of tribunician power, three-times consul, father of his country, the *civitas* of the Cornovii erected this.'

which reflect the differing character and needs of their inhabitants. Apart from settlements, we find a wide range of military, industrial and religious sites and burial places. These were set in a landscape that was heavily exploited. Britain was not dominated by primeval woodland but had a largely open landscape littered with farmsteads, and parcelled into small fields and coppiced woods which were farmed in a pattern not dissimilar to that which existed until the agricultural revolution of the eighteenth century. Our prime archaeological evidence is this human landscape.

Much can be inferred about the landscape from detailed observation and recording, through survey and the use of techniques such as aerial photography. Indeed, the evidence used to reconstruct the changing landscape comes from these sources alone. However, as the same tracts of countryside have been used for several thousands of years, layer upon layer of evidence is superimposed on it with features from each successive phase overwriting and partly obscuring earlier traces. The result is sometimes described as like a palimpsest – a parchment that has been reused after the previous writing has been erased leaving only faint traces.

Detailed information about settlements is provided by surveys and, in particular, by excavations in which individual sites are systematically dissected by archaeologists. These reveal the sequence of occupation and give insights into how the buried deposits accumulated. They provide a mute and partial history of the place since many past actions will have left no trace.

Activities at particular sites can be related to those elsewhere only by being tied to an historical timescale. This usually relies on an analysis of the objects found. We are fortunate that a wide variety of items was in use during the Roman period, especially as we can estimate the date of use for many of them. These objects are disparate and have been dated by a range of different specialist methods.

Least common, but perhaps of most value, are monumental stone or bronze inscriptions (**12**). Their purpose was varied but tombstones, altars and slabs recording building works are the most frequently found. They often contain information that enables us to relate them directly or indirectly to the Roman calendar. Inscriptions, however, are only very occasionally found in their original locations as many were later reused in other buildings. Although rarely of use for dating features on sites, they provide invaluable information for reconstructing the history of the province. As sources of information about military history, administrative organization and religious observances they are particularly important.

Less formal written sources are more commonly found on excavations although the writings are usually confined to single words or names written or scratched on everyday objects like pottery. These have limited value but may provide important social insights.

Less durable are the archives of official and personal documents written on wooden tablets, which have been excavated at the Roman town at Carlisle and the fort at Vindolanda near Hadrian's Wall (**13**). The Vindolanda texts contain information that dates them to the end of the first and the beginning of the second century AD. They were written in ink or scratched into wax on small, wafer-thin wooden writing-tablets. They survived by being buried in waterlogged conditions where oxygen had been excluded by the damp environment and normal biological decay thus arrested. This archive is of the greatest historical interest especially for the insights it provides about the everyday workings of the army.

Far more common as finds are coins. Roman coins do not bear dates, but their legends list the official titles and offices held by emperors, often for short periods of known duration. Through these the date that a coin was minted can often be established. This sometimes enables an archaeologist finding a coin on an excavation to establish the date of the feature in which it was found. As coins circulated for long periods and are susceptible to redeposition, for

13 *(above)* A wooden writing-tablet found at Vindolanda on the northern frontier and dated to around the end of the first century AD. It derives from the archive of the fort's garrison and provides an exceptional insight into life on the frontier. The text reads in translation: 'The Britons are unprotected by armour. There are very many cavalry. The cavalry do not use swords nor do the wretched Britons mount in order to throw javelins.'

instance in the footings of a later building, a date derived from a coin can usually only tell the archaeologist a range of time *after which* the context containing it was deposited. Although both closely dated and relatively common, coins thus provide less precise dating than might be expected. Like inscriptions, however, their legends and designs are a rich source for understanding political events and their large numbers enable inferences to be drawn about the economic history of the province (**14**).

Most objects commonly found on excavations are not themselves intrinsically datable. An average site will none the less produce a handful of metal objects (building and furniture fittings, personal ornaments, household equipment and utensils); a mass of fragmentary ceramic vessels; building debris; and food refuse, principally animal bones. These finds are often the most valuable in providing archaeologists with information about past lifestyles and past economies.

Sites, too, may be associated with historical events, particularly military campaigns, so the objects found on them provide a source for the comparative dating of finds from elsewhere. We broadly understand the history of construction, alteration and abandonment of Hadrian's Wall so artefacts found in particular phases of activity there can frequently be assigned a date. Closely similar artefacts found elsewhere can then also be ascribed to a similar date. Used with care, such dating evidence is important and remains vital to much work in the Roman period.

In areas like much of Scotland, which remained outside the empire for a long period, archaeologists face a different task. Large volumes and wide varieties of artefacts are generally absent and the only materials found, such as household pottery, changed little in style over very long periods and so are very difficult to date. Archaeologists thus use other methods for dating these sites. Changes in the forms of settlement site sometimes enable broad dates to be established for different styles of building. Excavators also rely heavily on techniques of absolute dating founded on the principles of atomic physics: namely, radiocarbon and luminescence dating. Within the short time-span covered by the Roman period such methods do not make it possible to arrive at a very refined dating and this makes comparison with historical events rather problematical. For instance, it is rarely possible to

14 *(above)* Coin of Antoninus Pius (AD 138–61) showing the seated figure Britannia on the reverse. This particular coin was issued in AD 154–5 and the depiction of Britannia is evidence of the celebration of a military victory in the province at this time.

establish whether a particular change took place *before* or *after* the beginning of the Roman occupation and thus whether or not it was caused by their arrival.

In the last few decades there has been a breakthrough in dating, using tree rings. This tree-ring dating, or dendrochronology, has already had a major impact on sites within the Roman province such as London and Carlisle (**15**). Given a good-sized piece of oak, we can establish when it grew and, if the youngest surviving ring is from just below the bark, estimate precisely its felling date. This method has enabled specialists to date timber surviving from Roman buildings with undreamt-of accuracy.

A site deserted in the Roman period will not survive unaltered to the present day. Differential survival means that excavations generally produce large quantities of robust materials like pottery and animal bone but little or no wood or textile. Exceptionally wet or very dry conditions arrest decay and allow organic materials to survive. It is the wet conditions that concern us particularly in Britain. Objects buried in a continuously waterlogged environment are protected from decay as the water excludes oxygen, which is necessary for organic decay to take place. Wet deposits, like those excavated since the 1970s in London, York and Carlisle, preserve a much wider range of material than is normally found, including botanical remains such as seeds as well as wooden artefacts (**16**). Such excavations, therefore, can provide a much clearer picture of life in the past than would otherwise be seen, but even here the evidence is not unaltered, for, in addition to the processes of physical decay, we have to contend with human agencies of destruction.

Except in unusual circumstances, such as the destruction of a site in an unexpected catastrophe, human beings rarely abandon sites intact. Most archaeological excavations deal with material either accidentally lost, deliberately deposited or left behind because it is no longer of value. Understanding excavated sites is easiest when we find evidence for the fixtures and fittings of a building: for instance metalworking hearths, which are immovable and leave us a clear indication of what was happening at a particular stage in a site's use. Even so, building uses do change and fittings become redundant, so the intended function may be entirely different from its later use. This demonstrates the importance of understanding the *processes* of development if we wish to interpret

15 *(above)* Photograph showing a section of the riverside wall of Roman London as excavated in 1975. In the foreground can be seen the wooden piles used for the foundations. These were originally covered by chalk before the stone wall, visible in the background, was built upon them. Tree-ring dating shows that the oak trees used for the piles were felled between AD 255 and 270.

sites properly. Even a site which is physically well preserved is likely to have been altered by human actions, both at the time of deposition and subsequently.

In addition, the archaeologist's own pattern of information gathering can add further distortions. Some archaeological sites are more visible than others and some areas more intensively studied. A settlement site that has been heavily damaged by past ploughing is more likely to be found by field reconnaissance or aerial photography if it lies in an area of arable agriculture than if it lies under pasture and, in both instances, it is only going to appear in the archaeological record when it is noted by an archaeologist. Hence, the distribution of known sites is also often heavily influenced by the distribution of archaeologists.

Archaeological evidence is inanimate and therefore mute. Unlike a written document the archaeological evidence cannot lie, but equally it cannot speak for itself and can only yield information through our interpretation. As already noted, although only an accidental by-product of past human activity, much archaeological evidence is not totally devoid of patterning and so is analogous to an encoded language. Some of this patterning has obvious meanings: the organization of space in architecture and town-plans, for example, is often closely related to social organization. The central and dominant position of the principal public building (the forum) in a Roman town shows us how the town was used as a political and social focus. Elsewhere, the concepts we are trying to understand are more subtle and vary both from place to place as well as through time, so that they remain a puzzle. The variety of careful ways in which human bodies were laid out in Romano-British cemeteries shows that importance was attached to details like the positioning of the hands. Although these patterns of positioning are observed repeatedly, the meaning of the symbolism remains obscure. Decoding meanings like these through comparisons with other societies is demanding and often contentious but provides a fascinating aspect of our research.

Sometimes, however, it appears deceptively easy to 'read' these patterns. Indeed, one of the challenges of dealing with material from the Roman world is its apparent familiarity. This has encouraged people to assume a similarity of outlook between us and the Romans; a child today may go into a museum and immediately

16 *(above)* Photograph showing detail of the bone inlay used to decorate a fourth-century wooden cupboard door found in a well at Hayton in East Yorkshire. The remarkable survival of the wood is a result of its burial in waterlogged deposits.

relate to many Roman objects because they appear familiar. This very familiarity can make us less aware than we ought to be of variations in outlook between us and those in the past, and amid the different peoples who lived within the empire. We cannot simply view Roman Britain through modern eyes and look for similarities. A wide variety of cultural differences lies between us and those who lived almost 2000 years ago. The challenge of archaeology involves adopting methods for understanding its otherworldliness in ways that we can share with anyone who cares to look at the evidence.

As we have seen, the basic work of the archaeologist involves examining our information, identifying patterns and interpreting them. Given the infinite range of the surviving material, which reflects a multitude of past activities, the task is never dull and we have the advantage over documentary historians of being able to excavate if we need fresh evidence.

When we move beyond the individual site or landscape to look for broader patterns in past society as a whole, our methods have to broaden. On sites, an archaeologist's recording methods are like those of the observational scientist. When we look at broader trends and write history using evidence we have gleaned, personal attitudes and individual experience play an increasingly important role, for the accumulated evidence cannot tell its own story. The archaeologist has to draw upon a wide range of information to aid understanding. This is where the subject is at its most stimulating, for information from a range of sources including the Classical texts and the anthropology of other societies has to be blended with our own evidence to paint a realistic picture. The best interpretations are those that most satisfactorily explain our observations, and the most robust are those that remain valid as new evidence is collected. Outsiders may feel unsettled by the uncertainties introduced in such a rapidly changing discipline but for me this provides much of the subject's attraction.

1 THE PEOPLES OF BRITAIN

A full appreciation of Britain during its period of contact with the Roman Empire must begin with a realization that its inhabitants were diverse and grouped into a variety of different, generally small-scale tribes. There was no single communal identity that unified those living in these islands. The concept of 'Britons' was imposed by Mediterranean peoples in the way modern Western society has conflated all indigenous South Americans as 'Indians'.

Our knowledge of these communities is affected by the limited geographical knowledge of those living in the Classical world and the incomplete survival of the relevant sources. The recorded names of the more far-flung peoples also changed as they developed through the period. Although details are very difficult to understand, we can observe a broad evolution over five centuries. Just beyond the boundaries of the empire, continual Roman diplomatic and military intervention upset social stability, so any static picture of the peoples of Britain is misleading.

Our knowledge is largely derived from literary sources and varies with the extent of exposure to Rome, so I have grouped Britain (and Ireland) into four broad zones. Southern and eastern England were influenced by Rome from an early date and were in close contact from the middle of the first century BC. They subsequently became the core of the urbanized Roman province. Wales and the west and north of England were less directly affected until after the conquest of AD 43 when they too gradually came under Rome's influence. Although eventually annexed, the institutions of Roman civil administration did not become as well established there as in the south and east and the Roman army continued in occupation for centuries. In southern and central Scotland, Rome campaigned periodically and persistently attempted to exercise diplomatic control. Largely beyond Rome's reach lay northern and western Scotland and Ireland.

Settled agricultural communities had been present in Britain for over two thousand years and the climate was broadly similar to that of today, although perhaps marginally warmer. Most of the native woodland had been cleared for agriculture and much that remained consisted of stands of small trees with multiple stems, which were periodically cut and used for products such as wattles or charcoal. This open landscape was parcelled into small fields divided by hedges and ditches, or by dry-stone walls.

Varying agricultural potential distinguished different areas. The lowlands of eastern England show evidence for later Iron Age arable expansion on to lands that were more difficult to cultivate. Arable agriculture was also practised in upland areas, but limited by the availability of suitable land. The distribution of farmsteads in such areas as Northumberland, which are moorland today, suggests that farming was in an expansive phase, with cultivation moving beyond its present limits.

The upland topography limited the size of the communities and restricted their contacts with one another. It is all too easy to forget that difficulties in communication had a profound effect on the nature of earlier societies. Even on Roman roads, travel was slow and treacherous. Away from the roads overland transport by foot or pack animal was limited and often perilous. Transport by water was more rapid and reliable, but regular sea voyages generally only took place between March and October. River transport was especially important for the movement of bulky goods. Goods and information travelled slowly, and most of the population were probably never aware of the historical events previously outlined.

Evidence from other societies suggests that there was little migration of people even where towns developed. Most country dwellers rarely strayed far from their homes and seldom met outsiders. This engendered a strong local social cohesion, which accounts for the stable character of settlement in many areas but it also created a problem for Rome as native peoples' loyalties were primarily local. The key to Roman success was in engendering an identity of interest between Rome's aspirations and those of the local leaders.

SOUTHERN AND EASTERN ENGLAND

The peoples here were in the process of evolving towards a centralized social organization at the time of the Roman conquest and their groupings consequently vary in both size and sophistication. Organization was generally centred on small clans, several of which coalesced into larger tribes under the leadership of either a single chief or, more occasionally, pairs of magistrates. Larger groupings had often been initiated at times of war when loose bonds linking the clans had hardened into more formal alliances in

17 *(right)* Map of southern England and Wales in the Late Iron Age. The squares represent probable *oppida* (large lowland sites) and are shown against the background of the regional coinage distributions, which have been labelled using the tribal names as known after the conquest of AD 43. The Celtic place-names of these *oppida* are shown where they are known from the coins.

the face of adversity. From the middle of the first century BC intertribal rivalries were becoming more intense, and the resulting conflicts probably led to these informal groupings becoming more permanent. Rapid changes occurred as tribal territories expanded and shifting alliances led clans to split off and create new groupings. Tribal organization only became fossilized after AD 43 with Rome's *de facto* recognition of the groups with whom she had come into contact. This became institutionalized as Rome made treaties and incorporated their territories into the Roman system as *civitates*.

A key issue in this complex period is how far the Roman presence in Gaul after Caesar's conquest in the 50s BC destabilized the British tribes, upsetting the balances of power within native societies as Rome lent her support to British leaders with whom she had diplomatic contacts.

In southeast England events during the later Iron Age are dimly discernible through the evidence of native coinages. The tribes most directly influenced by Rome had started to use coins imported from Gaul by the beginning of the first century BC. Subsequently they minted their own coins, some of which were inscribed with the names of rulers or places (**17, 18**). The sequence of their issue enables us to reconstruct the history of the different rulers, some of whom are mentioned by Classical writers. These coins are found

18 *(above)* Iron Age gold coin of Cunobelinus minted *c.* AD 10–25. The inscription 'CAMV' refers to Camulodunon (Colchester), whilst 'CVNO' is an abbreviation of the ruler's name. Careful plotting of the distribution of finds of coins like these, which bear names of Late Iron Age leaders, enables archaeologists to reconstruct something of the tribal territories and political history of the period.

across circumscribed territories that are almost mutually exclusive, so it is inferred that only the coins of the local tribe were generally used within its territory. The distribution of finds of coins indicates the changing territories of the tribes during the decades before the Roman invasion.

Other features also differentiate these tribes from those elsewhere in Britain. Everything suggests that they were increasingly evolving more marked and enduring class differences. The speed of this evolution varied between tribes. Those in the Essex–Hertfordshire area apparently led, and there was a progressively later start with distance to the west and north. Other features that illustrate developing social stratification are the growth of the larger permanent settlements, the appearance of graves richly furnished with luxury goods, and the production and use of prestige luxury items such as highly decorated metalwork. In addition, the increased use of imported Roman objects and commodities was confined to a few settlements. Later, on the eve of the conquest, the wider distribution of Roman goods indicates a change towards more commercialized relations, with continental traders taking advantage of the appetites whetted by earlier diplomatic gifts. Such contacts emerged especially as the adjacent areas of northern Gaul became increasingly Roman in character during the first half of the first century AD.

Settlement evidence also exhibits important changes in the period leading up to the conquest. The basic pattern of settlement comprised farmsteads and hamlets set in a landscape of small, so-called Celtic fields. The farmsteads varied in size from single houses to small clusters, with a few larger nucleations. They were fairly densely distributed, for where we have good evidence from detailed archaeological surveys, settlements are often found about every kilometre although there remained areas that were more sparsely occupied. It is no coincidence that the boundaries between some tribes follow natural features, so that the social groups were partly bounded by the natural environment that they occupied.

The farm buildings, including the houses, were generally round in plan, and had cone-shaped roofs of thatch (**19**). Smaller square buildings also occurred and were most likely granaries. The circular style of building should not lead us to think of the houses as mere huts, for this underestimates both their scale and sophistication.

19 *(above)* Reconstruction of the experimental Iron Age farmstead at Butser, Hampshire. The large roundhouse within an earthwork enclosure gives an impression of how a typical lowland settlement might have appeared on the eve of the Roman conquest.

20 *(below)* An exceptionally well-preserved Roman timber building, probably a warehouse, excavated in Southwark, London. Waterlogged conditions had preserved the timbers of the floor of this building, probably a warehouse, the methods of construction of which are probably typical of the period. The fashion for rectangular rather than circular buildings first spread to Britain in the first century BC. Tree-ring dating shows that this building was constructed *c.* AD 152.

These were spectacular houses, often as large in floor area as many modern ones, and their constructional techniques illustrate a fine empirical appreciation of engineering. The roofs of the largest houses were frequently 15m (50ft) across and thus their height would have been the same measurement, so they must have been an imposing sight, dominating the landscape and providing a very visible sign of the status of the occupier. Towards the time of the Roman conquest, a few new types of rectangular timber building began to be constructed, mainly in the larger settlements of the southeast. This marks the introduction of a new architectural tradition that relied on joinery techniques similar to those familiar to us from medieval timber-framed houses (**20, 21**).

Farmsteads throughout the region were often enclosed by a bank and ditch, sometimes of formidable proportions. The ditches were frequently more than 1m (3ft) deep and usually had a palisade or earthen bank around their inside edge which combined to form a very substantial obstacle. These served partly to exclude stock or to hold them within the yard, but as this could equally have been achieved with a thorn hedge or fence, the enclosures probably also served to display the status of the owners and define their territory. This also indicates that land was effectively privately controlled by this stage in the evolution of southern and eastern Britain.

Within this landscape were some larger settlements. Over most of this region the hilltop enclosures, known as hill-forts, common in the earlier Iron Age had fallen out of use. However, in some areas such as the territory of the Durotriges centred on Dorset, they remained in use and some contained large concentrations of roundhouses within their substantial defensive enclosures (**23**). Some perhaps acted as foci for the clans who merged to form the confederation of the Durotriges in time of war. Others probably acted as periodic meeting-places and religious centres, and even communal granaries where a tribe's surplus could be kept, but their inhospitable locations and the limited evidence for their permanent occupation confirm that we should not think of them as towns.

Around the beginning of the first century AD a number of other diverse focal settlements came into existence. These sites, generally in river valleys, are somewhat misleadingly referred to by the Latin term *oppidum*, loosely meaning 'town'. However, the newly established settlements in Britain were neither very similar to one

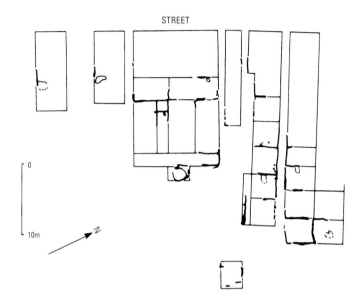

STREET

21 *(right)* Simplified plan of a group of timber buildings of *c.* AD 90, demolished in order to make way for the construction of the forum in London. They are typical of the timber artisans' houses found in the earlier Romano-British towns.

another nor do they closely resemble those on the Continent which are described using the same word. They are also very different from the towns of the contemporary Mediterranean world.

The largest in England was Camulodunon (Camulodunum in Latin) at Colchester, the tribal capital of the Catuvellauni at the time of the conquest, where a vast area of about 30 sq km (11.6 sq miles) was defined by a complex series of discontinuous earthen dykes. Inside were a series of centres of activity, some also enclosed within their own earthworks (**22**). One was certainly a temple, another a settlement and there was also an industrial area. This site was the tribal centre, since coins bear its name and it was the primary target for the Roman campaign of conquest under Claudius in AD 43. Other sites, such as Braughing in Hertfordshire, were not surrounded by massive earthworks but shared other of their features, implying that we are witnessing the emergence of a range of new types of important settlement. Some were the capitals of emergent tribes and their growth probably resulted from the increasingly stratified nature of society and political centralization. This was the outcome of both internal conflict between the native peoples of the region and external diplomatic contacts with the Roman world. This social evolution involved an upward spiral of competition between tribes as they fought to gain dominance over territories and peoples. Success attracted traders from abroad, who supplied the material goods that enabled leaders to display their

22 *(right)* Simplified plan of the Late Iron Age *oppidum* at Colchester. The site consisted of a large territory between two rivers that was defined by earthworks. Within this area there were a series of centres of activity. Among these were the temple at Gosbecks and the industrial complex at Sheepen. The settlement was the target of the first stage of the Claudian invasion and continued in occupation (with the Latinized name Camulodunum). First a Roman legionary fortress, then a *colonia* were built here within a decade of the conquest ensuring that it remained a key settlement within the Roman province.

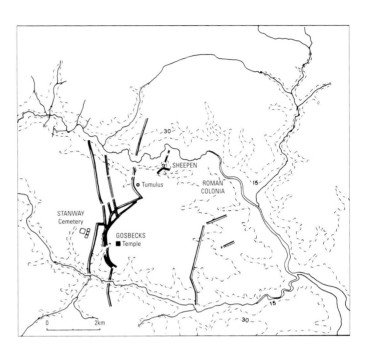

dominance by the use of the exotic goods over which they held a virtual monopoly. Local manufacture also became closely associated with these new focal sites. These societies were in a flux of change, and competition resulted in their central settlements and forms of social display being transformed to more closely resemble those in neighbouring Roman Gaul. Indeed the adjacent Roman presence destabilized the balances of native power. Changes might anyway have taken place, but their speed and ferocity in the region nearest the Continent certainly resulted from Roman proximity. Events in this region had a knock-on effect on life beyond the southeast. Alterations in agricultural production resulted from the increased demands for food from the growing non-productive population of warriors, craftworkers and nobility. Slaves were supplied to the empire in unknown numbers (**24**). These captives, like some of the commodities traded with Rome such as gold and silver, probably came from beyond the areas in direct contact with the Continent.

WALES, WESTERN AND NORTHERN ENGLAND

These areas were eventually incorporated into the empire but remained marginal to the developed province, with only limited evidence for the growth of villas and towns. In the later Iron Age

23 *(above)* Aerial photograph showing the Iron Age hill-fort of Hod Hill in Dorset. The large earthworks defining the settlement on the top of the hill are clearly visible together with the Roman fort inserted in the corner of the enclosure to enable a unit of soldiers to watch over the native population soon after the invasion of AD 43.

24 *(below)* Gang slave chain from the Iron Age hill-fort at Bigberry in Kent. Similar chains and single manacles have been found widely around the peripheries of the Roman Empire indicating a trade in slaves to supply Rome's needs. Conflict associated with such trade probably brought about considerable changes in native society as the empire expanded.

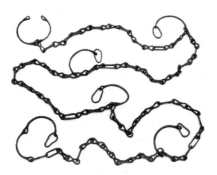

they were peripheral to those areas in direct contact with the Roman world. Therefore they effectively form the boundary zone separating Roman influence from the regions which the Romans saw as barbarian. These areas were not unchanging, but the dynamics of development were internally driven rather than externally stimulated.

Their physical geography is dominated by uplands and moors with only comparatively small pockets of hospitable land. There is strong evidence, however, for a fairly substantial population, with a prevalence of sites enclosed within earthwork compounds (**25**). The enclosures comprise a range wider than found in the south and east. Like the farmsteads there, these compounds commonly contained roundhouses, although they often had dry-stone or earthen walls. This style of farmstead remained common throughout the period of Roman occupation, for there were very few Romanized sites such as villas and small towns. Where these did occur most were close to the more developed parts of the province on the lower lands. The farmsteads themselves did change and some also received a limited range and quantity of Roman-style goods. The small number of goods, even when the south and east were flooded with them, suggests that these areas were less integrated into the Roman system. The contrast is particularly striking when comparisons are made with the military forts that were often situated in the same areas for long periods. These were always rich in material goods, but excavations on nearby farmsteads rarely recover more than the odd Roman glass bead or piece of pottery. The overwhelming impression is that the Roman military and the traditional native systems existed independently side by side. In many cases, it appears that the indigenous peoples deliberately rejected material symbols associated with Rome.

25 *(above)* Aerial photograph of the native rural settlement site at Thorpe Thewles in Cleveland. A sub-rectangular ditched enclosure containing a roundhouse is clearly visible. Such farmsteads are very common in the later Iron Age settlements of northern England.

26 *(below)* Aerial photograph of the 'round' near Constantine, Cornwall. The settlement was surrounded by a circular earthwork bank, marked by a modern hedge. Such enclosured settlements are typical of the native farmsteads of Cornwall and are similar to those found in Wales and elsewhere in the west.

Further contrast is provided by the continued use of hill-forts. Their distribution shows very marked local differences with some areas, such as Wales, thickly covered, while in others, such as Cornwall and Northumbria, they are more sparse. Their size varies considerably. In Wales the numerous small hill-forts, generally of little more than 1 ha (2.5 acres) in extent and containing roundhouses, were the dominant settlement type and not merely defended retreats. Given their small scale and the nature of the terrain they were probably the equivalent of the farmsteads found in the lowlands. This too is the impression created by the settlement patterns in Cornwall. The dominant settlement type there was the circular or sub-rectangular enclosed farmstead of about 1 ha, locally called the 'round' (**26**), although there was also a limited number of larger enclosures that perhaps acted as local centres. A similar pattern appears in parts of west Wales, where such farmsteads are referred to as 'raths', and equally over much of Cumbria and Northumberland.

We should be cautious about concluding that these areas were socially unsophisticated. One of the clear lessons of anthropology is that complex and highly differentiated societies often have settlements that do not betray this. The impression created by the archaeology of these areas is of a society without obvious social hierarchy. However, differences in rank may have been largely confined within the extended family or local group and expressed in a manner that has left little archaeological trace. The size of someone's herd of cattle or their right to the first helping at dinner could have communicated their social position in these smaller-scale societies as it certainly did in later Celtic societies.

Northern England and central and north Wales experienced long-term military occupation. In Wales Rome had extreme difficulty in subduing the native tribes, so a substantial garrison was left to oversee the population and guard resources such as the gold mines until well into the Roman period, with some forts remaining in occupation into the fourth century. Northern England remained as a frontier zone. It faced an area which not only lay outside the province but which was also the object of Rome's continuing territorial ambitions. Between campaigns, a substantial garrison remained billeted in forts throughout the region, with especial concentrations along the linear frontiers built and reconstituted by successive emperors from the 120s onwards (**27, 28, 29**).

This garrison in northern England varied in size during the different stages of the occupation, but its enormous scale is indicated by the estimate that it comprised some 26,410 men under the Emperor Hadrian (see **7**). Such numbers must have had a substantial impact on the area, although they were unevenly spread. The army was divided into units of varying size with the strategic reserve of two legions, of about 5000 men each, based some distance behind the frontier (at York and Chester). Units were stationed both on the frontier and in forts forward and behind it, located to maintain command of the communications network. Settlements outside the fort gates (see **62**) and outside the garrison towns at Carlisle and Corbridge were dominated by foreigners. The incomers made considerable demands on the local area if only for food, pasture and fuel. The zone remained under military control, so native lands and lifestyles were disrupted. The very presence of a substantial number of young, foreign males will also have upset the social balance of the community.

In northern England the army had a negative effect on native society. Prior to the invasion this region had a similar pattern of settlement to areas further south. Elsewhere such a pattern prefigured successful self-government under the Romans after a brief interlude during which the invading armies had passed through. In northeast England this might also have been the pattern but the gradual withdrawal of the Roman army from Scotland through the later first century was followed by the construction of a frontier across the region. The normal pattern whereby Rome handed control of civil affairs to indigenous leaders did not take place and the region remained under military rule. This robbed the local nobility of any opportunity to gain and maintain social prestige or accumulate wealth. Instead the native elite, the natural allies of

Rome in her oligarchic system of government, were forced into subservience. This was socially destructive and almost certainly explains the failure of northern England to develop a rich pattern of villas and towns. It was also perhaps the cause of the ill-understood violent troubles that afflicted the north during the second half of the second century. Such violent revolts often characterize people disenchanted and frustrated in their ambitions who lack an identity of interest with those controlling society.

SOUTHERN AND CENTRAL SCOTLAND

Southern Scotland, including the central Lowlands, was first incorporated within the empire by Agricola, but then largely evacuated (see **6–9**). A few forts along communication lines into the region continued in occupation. Rome maintained diplomatic contacts and presumably constant military patrolling and intelligence gathering. The four tribes who occupied the area seem not to have presented a significant threat to Roman interests and Roman power had no very obvious impact on them.

On the eve of Roman intervention there were strong similarities between the patterns of settlement in these parts of southern Scotland and those of northern and western England. A rich and varied settlement pattern was maintained, although sites have received less attention from excavators than they deserve. There are a large number of small enclosures – of less than 0.5 ha (1.2 acres) – as well as unenclosed valley-slope settlements of a similar size dominated by timber roundhouses. Some of the former are on hilltop locations, but others (known as 'crannogs') are found on lake edges surrounded by shallow water. All these settlements were set within an agriculturally rich landscape that was widely cleared of woodland.

Among the defended settlements there was a limited number of larger hill-forts – more than c. 6 ha (15 acres) – the spectacular topographical locations and substantial earthen defences of which dominated their regions. The largest of these forts (Eildon Hill and Traprain Law) are up to 16 ha (40 acres) in extent, and clearly acted as major foci for the region (**30**). Their character implies some social centralization, but it is not always possible to associate particular hill-forts with the historically attested tribes (**31**).

The highly sophisticated sites like Traprain, together with the reasonably widespread distribution of Roman material on indigenous sites throughout the region, suggest that these areas of southern Scotland were the beneficiaries of the Roman presence further south. Instead of suffering from the imposition of a Roman military presence they experienced a period of alliance with either trade or the receipt of diplomatic gifts stimulating a period of development (**32**). We can see this region as a contrast to the areas of stunted indigenous development further south, for their local culture continued to flourish and evolve while in contact with the Roman province. There are also hints that developments in areas unfriendly to Rome were being manipulated by her familiar use of both force and diplomacy.

NORTHERN SCOTLAND AND IRELAND

Except for the briefest of encounters with the Roman military and occasional traders and travellers, some of whom circumnavigated these islands, the farther-flung areas of Britain were comparatively untouched by direct Roman intervention. This is not to say that they continued entirely unchanged. Both areas received modest numbers of Roman objects (**33, 34**), whether directly through trade or through intermediaries, while it should not be forgotten that it was via the Roman Empire that Christianity was eventually brought to Ireland in the early fifth century.

It was most likely the continuing Roman presence to the south and her repeated interventions that stimulated changes in the organization of the northern Scottish tribes. An aspect of Roman control beyond the frontier is illustrated by the written sources for the decades around the end of the second century when the Caledonians

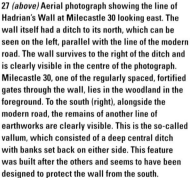

27 *(above)* Aerial photograph showing the line of Hadrian's Wall at Milecastle 30 looking east. The wall itself had a ditch to its north, which can be seen on the left, parallel with the line of the modern road. The wall survives to the right of the ditch and is clearly visible in the centre of the photograph. Milecastle 30, one of the regularly spaced, fortified gates through the wall, lies in the woodland in the foreground. To the south (right), alongside the modern road, the remains of another line of earthworks are clearly visible. This is the so-called vallum, which consisted of a deep central ditch with banks set back on either side. This feature was built after the others and seems to have been designed to protect the wall from the south.

28 *(above right)* View of the central section of Hadrian's Wall seen from the west looking towards Housesteads fort. This is the part of the wall which has survived best where one can see the curtain-wall standing up to 2 m (6 ft) in height.

29 *(right)* Aerial photograph of the fort on Hadrian's Wall at Housesteads from the north. Hadrian's Wall can be seen joining the fort wall at the bottom left-hand corner. The excavated buildings within the fort, barracks, granaries, the headquarters building and the commanding officer's house are clearly visible and unexcavated structures can be detected as earthworks. Buildings of the *vicus* outside the south gate can be seen at the top of the photograph.

30 *(below)* The hill-fort of Traprain Law in southern Scotland. This partly quarried hill was evidently an important centre within the tribal territory of the Votadini, one of Rome's neighbours beyond Hadrian's Wall. This site has produced a range of imported Roman goods and a hoard of later Roman silver.

breached a treaty with Rome and revolted. Rome's military attentions were engaged elsewhere, so the tribe of the Maeatae were bought off with a bribe, which obtained peace until renewed trouble led to an invasion under Septimius Severus (208–11). Diplomatic gifts were used by Rome to buy off tribes behind those on the border who kept their neighbours under pressure and thus in check. Over a sustained period this may have encouraged social centralization (see **32**). Where this was not followed by conquest, it ensured both tribal dependence on Rome and further potential instability when subsidies ceased to be paid or there were changes among those in power. Such was the history of northern Scotland, that increased unity and power came at the stage when Roman Britain was internally weakened and unable either to conquer and absorb the rest of the island, or effectively repel military incursions. The indirect stimulus of Rome on the Scottish populations had a direct effect on the barbarian incursions, which played a significant part in the eventual destruction of Roman Britain itself.

POPULATION

A broad understanding of the economy and its organization are vital for they show what Britain offered the imperial power. To understand the economy we need to estimate the size of the population, although we can never be precise in a period before appropriate documentary records survive. One approach is to work from settlement distributions since the whole country was reasonably heavily occupied. Not all sites were occupied at the same time, and the quality of evidence is variable, but there is sound evidence that in rich arable areas there was commonly one settlement per square kilometre (250 acres) at the height of the Roman period. Given the

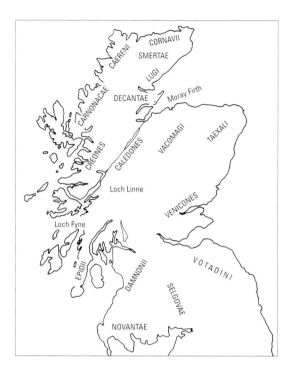

31 *(above)* Map of the tribes known in Scotland from Ptolemy's account in the mid-second century AD. His sources probably date to the time of Agricola's expeditions 70 years earlier.

32 *(above right)* Map of Scottish tribes in the third century AD. The reduction in the number of tribes compared with those known in the first century may be the result of centralization and changes in social organization stimulated by contacts with Rome.

total area of farmland in England and Wales we can estimate an original total of about 100,000 settlement sites. A comparable figure for Ireland, simply based on the number of known ring-forts, may be 40,000 and we guess at a similar number of sites in Scotland. There may have been as many as 180,000 rural settlements in Britain before any allowance is made for the larger sites.

The translation of this rough estimate into a population figure is fraught with difficulties, not least because of the need to make assumptions about the social organization of the inhabitants. Although information about Celtic family structure is found in medieval sources, we cannot assume either that it is applicable to our period or that the different tribes were organized in the same way. Nevertheless it suggests that the extended family group was common. In contrast to the nuclear family, such households held several generations who shared a common ancestor – the great-grandfather in the Irish custom. In this tradition, the community occupying a single farmstead may often have numbered over 20.

Taking 20 as an estimate we obtain a total rural population of the British Isles of 3.6 million. This estimate, however, gives too static an impression of a population whose size undoubtedly fluctuated. Variations in population cannot be seen in the archaeological evidence unless we can distinguish between the abandonment of

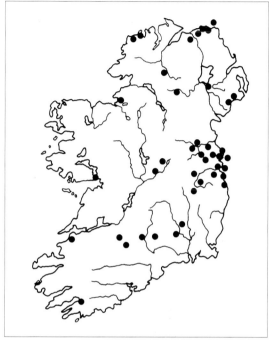

33 *(above)* Map showing the distribution of Roman objects in Scotland. Although rather crude, this gives a clear impression of the scale of Roman contacts.

34 *(above right)* Map showing the distribution of Roman objects in Ireland. The rather sparse distribution compares with that of Scotland to the north of the Antonine Wall.

sites and their failure to participate in the economy that supplied archaeologically datable artefacts. We suspect that the peaceful period of Roman control witnessed population growth but our evidence does not allow us to document such a trend.

It is easier to calculate the size of other portions of the population. We know from the written evidence that the Roman army varied from a peak of about 55,000 down to perhaps 10,000–20,000 in the fourth century. Allowing for their dependants, their number may have amounted to perhaps 125,000. Equally, we can measure the total area occupied by the Roman towns. Given comparative evidence of urban population densities we estimate up to 240,000 townspeople. These precise numbers are not important, but they give a clear indication of population balance and show that even within the Roman province people not engaged in farming and therefore supported by others' production accounted for less than one in ten of the population. The overall pattern is of a primarily agrarian economy, characteristic of preindustrial Europe, with the proportion of the population dependent on commerce or manufacturing remaining very small and the scale of their enterprises comparatively modest. This economy need not have been undeveloped, but its emphasis was very different to that of the modern Western world.

AGRICULTURE

Agriculturally the Roman period continued a phase that began around 1000 BC. The agrarian economy was dominated by mixed farming, with a variety of domestic stock and cereal crops. The full range of domesticated animals was exploited, although the breeds raised were different from those of today. Cattle were considerably smaller in stature, and sheep had not then been selectively bred for the large and fluffy fleeces familiar today. The cereal crops grown (wheat, barley and rye) were also varieties of those familiar from the modern hybrids. However, the emphasis of agriculture was different, with the hardier strains of emmer wheat preferred to the bread wheats grown today. Most obviously the fields would have looked different because they were not kept clear of weeds through the use of chemicals. Instead the cereals grew with and competed against weeds, so the fields would have appeared as a riot of summer colour. The spread of this agricultural regime across Britain was followed in the later Iron Age and into the Roman period by more intensive use of existing land and increased exploitation of heavier and more marginal soils. These trends illustrate a continued increase in demand for foodstuffs generated by either an expanding population or the increasing needs for consumption within society.

Agricultural innovation characterized the period immediately preceding the Roman conquest of southern Britain, and although a number of new features were introduced afterwards these were associated with the storage and processing of crops rather than their production. The later Iron Age agricultural economy was sufficiently developed to support Roman demands, at least in the south of England. Changes in stock at this time included the introduction of larger animals, while the arrival of sheep with superior fleeces may have started in the Iron Age rather than after the arrival of the Romans. Another phase of improvements, in ploughing and harvesting technology, occurred 150 years later than the conquest in the third and fourth centuries (**35**). A gradual shift in animal husbandry throughout the Roman period saw a decreasing reliance on sheep and an increasing emphasis on cattle. Such trends have important implications for the people's diet and lifestyle but cannot simply be explained as a result of Roman agricultural improvements. They were part of the longer-term agricultural evolution that originated long before our period.

35 *(right)* Small bronze model of a plough from Piercebridge, Co. Durham. Although often taken as an image of Romano-British agriculture, this statuette is actually religious in character, showing the ploughing of a sacred boundary around a settlement. The two animals yoked are a cow and a bull. Ploughing of the first sod to define the boundary would have moved anticlockwise around the settlement. In this way the bull, with its male attribute of strength, was on the outside defending the settlement, while the cow, symbolizing female fertility, was on the inward side, facing towards the community and representing the home. The ploughman as priest has his head covered with a hooded woollen cloak, perhaps the type known from ancient sources as the *birrus Britannicus*.

That a very prosperous agricultural regime existed is illustrated by Classical references to the export of grain during the first centuries BC and AD and again in the middle of the fourth century. The first-century source, Strabo, also mentions the export of hides from Britain, and at the beginning of the fourth century we learn of the export of a type of high-quality woollen cloak (the *birrus Britannicus*) (see **35**) and a form of saddle blanket (the *tapete Britannicum*). Provided that these items were exports, and not simply names of styles (like 'India Pale Ale'), these hint that other agricultural products also held a significant export market. That such exports should have occurred during the fourth century is significant since by this period the size of the agriculturally non-productive population needing to be fed and clothed was probably at its maximum. This certainly shows that Britain's considerable agricultural potential was exploited to great effect.

The wealth accumulated in many areas from the Late Iron Age onwards denotes that agriculture was productive throughout the period. The high-quality decorative metalwork and the great deposits of gold torcs and coins were the product of wealth accumulation by primarily agrarian communities. Equally, major public displays of affluence and status, such as villas, urban public buildings and temples characteristic of Romanized areas, were also the product of capital initially generated by tilling the land. That this was the case is shown by the social significance attached to land ownership in the ancient world. Access to the machinery of politics and power within the Roman system of government was limited to those who fulfilled a wealth qualification, measured by their control of land. In the areas of Britain that became urbanized under the Romans, the ownership of the primary means of production – the land – was the key to power.

The period thus saw the private ownership of the land, and by implication the tenancy of subject workers. This is illustrated by a legal text recording a land sale found at the Roman villa of Chew Stoke in Somerset and by a wooden tablet from London which concerns a property dispute in Kent. How far land outside the Romanized areas was communally owned is unknown. The common occurrence of defended farmsteads and enclosed fields implies control over land, but does not show whether it was owned individually or treated as a communal resource. We may do no more than guess that a fundamental distinction emerged between the Roman province, where the accumulation of private land holdings accompanied the emergence of an increasingly hierarchical society, and the areas outside, which retained traditional control of land as a community resource. A grey area certainly existed between the two extremes. The late Roman compilation of legal decisions, known as the Theodosian Code, records a case in Britain where Celtic laws of land ownership came into conflict with those of Rome.

Within the Roman province land was also treated as a commodity that could be owned by people from other provinces. In the year 404 a middle-ranking member of the aristocratic (or senatorial) class from Italy sold her lands, including properties in Britain, to benefit the church. The fourth century also witnessed the increasing practice throughout the empire obliging peasants *(coloni)* to remain on the lands where they worked so that they effectively became feudal serfs. A legal text of 20 November 319 confirms that Britain was affected by this change although we do not know how common it became. Removal of the control of land from those who farmed it marked the emergence of social inequality and the breakdown of the close kinship of family bonds that characterizes many agrarian societies. Although agriculture remained fundamental to wealth production, changes in its control within the Roman province illustrate a significant break from the previous pattern that persisted in the un-Romanized areas. This marks a very important stage in the social and economic history of Britain.

MANUFACTURE AND COMMERCE

Craft and manufacture were present in later prehistoric Britain as illustrated by the assortment of both spectacular metal objects for elite display and day-to-day items found on many excavations. These range from the pots and implements used in the household, to ornamental items of bone and wood that bear the same decorative features as found on metalwork. There are also hints that textiles were similarly decorated. These objects were mostly made of locally available materials. It is of little surprise that the designs represented by the shapes of pots had localized distributions. In other societies such local designs were symbols by which tribal identities were communicated to neighbouring peoples. It was thus perhaps possible to read a person's ethnic identity, their marital status and social rank from the patterns displayed in their everyday life, in much the same way that modern consumer goods betray social status and aspirations.

The volume of production of these objects was probably not large as even the biggest later Iron Age sites have not produced vast assemblages of durable finds. They also tend to be monotonous in character. The quantity and variety of things made from organic materials like wood and leather may have been greater, but too few waterlogged sites have been excavated for us to be sure. The small totals of objects from later Iron Age sites and their localized character imply that manufacture was generally organized within the household, with members of the family producing for themselves and the local community. The passing of craft skills from generation to generation ensured that styles and designs changed only slowly and encapsulated local traditions. Larger-scale production and distribution did take place. For instance, some widely distributed styles of pots have been shown to have been made at single locations. Late Iron Age pottery from the Glastonbury area was skilfully made and is found all across southern Britain, although the small numbers of finds show that they were not distributed commercially. Such products were probably obtained at occasional clan gatherings, through the exchange of gifts between allies, or even distributed by itinerant pedlars. Salt in particular was vital for the preservation of meat and its transport may have distributed other objects. Independent pedlars perhaps collected salt from the production centres and then traded it for other goods, which they exchanged further along a circuit that eventually returned to the salterns. Alternatively tribal leaders might have kept the trade under tight control because of the importance of salt to their people.

It is similarly difficult to understand the trade in goods of copper alloy (such as pins and brooches) and iron (principally

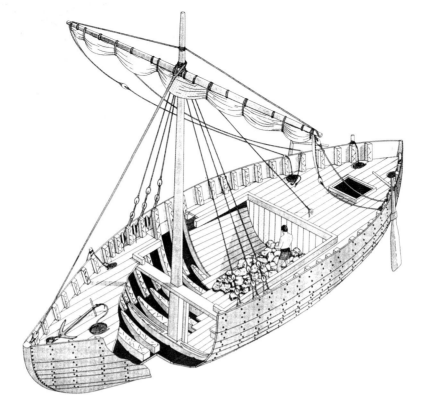

36 *(above)* Reconstruction of a Roman ship from Blackfriars in London that sank around the middle of the second century AD. At the time it was carrying a cargo of stone from Kent for building purposes. Ships like this one would have been common and were of crucial importance for the widespread trade that characterized the Roman period.

37 *(below)* Roman silver cup dated to the end of the first century BC found in a grave at Welwyn Garden City, Hertfordshire. Such imported objects probably came to Iron Age Britain as diplomatic gifts rather than as a result of trading. They show developing contacts between the native peoples and Rome in the period leading up to the invasion of AD 43.

brooches and tools) that arrived on a wide range of sites. Their styles show regional distributions and as there were only limited metal sources we infer specialist manufacture. Some metalworking, generally smithing, took place on a wide range of sites, so we should envisage travelling smiths and tinkers distributing new items, repairing the old, and removing scrap for recycling. The small numbers of metal artefacts found on ordinary sites show that the people were not a part of any large-scale consumer society.

Luxury goods, such as the imported wine, olive oil and fish brought from the Mediterranean world from the first century BC onwards (**36**), and the high-quality metal artefacts used for aristocratic display, had an even more limited distribution which was perhaps controlled by tribal aristocrats (**37**). Similarly the most highly specialized metalworkers presumably produced for these leaders. Their skills are obvious from the quality of the gold, silver and bronze that have survived from the period. Equally, precious-metal sources were probably controlled by a limited social group and although mining was not highly developed, knowledge of metal reserves was certainly available. Indeed iron, gold and silver were listed by Strabo as among Britain's exports at the end of the first century BC.

On the eve of Roman invasion we thus see a society in which the manufacturing economy had developed with its emphasis on the household and on craft skills, and where the best quality and greatest range of goods were largely a monopoly of the tribal aristocracies. Such an economy endured outside the Roman province although it grew to use some Roman goods. These Roman objects were mostly pots, glass vessels and small metal trinkets, which were dispersed over a broad area. They perhaps held a

38 *(right)* A pair of glass vessels found in the eastern cemetery of Roman London. The group dates to *c.* AD 150 and consists of a barrel-shaped bottle (the base of which is stamped with a maker's mark, FRONTSEXTIN), and a hexagonal bottle. Glass vessels were important for the transport of traded commodities but, unlike pottery, they could be melted down for reuse, so are less commonly found on archaeological sites. None the less they decrease frequency on sites in Britain after the conquest.

39 *(below)* A second-century pottery drinking vessel produced at kilns in the Nene valley near Peterborough and found on Hadrian's Wall. During the Roman period the mass-production of items like these flourished and skilled specialist workers were widespread throughout the area.

symbolic value and were not necessarily used for their originally designed purposes. The distribution of Roman goods outside the province in Britain does not seem to have happened on an enormous scale. Where objects occur in larger numbers, in the regional centres of southeast Scotland, they probably result from a special relationship between the tribes and the Roman government, which was cemented by the presentation of gifts.

In the areas that came under direct Roman control economic development is obvious. There was a vast increase in the number and variety of goods in circulation, and the range of settlements on which they are found. This is blindingly obvious on the vast majority of excavated sites in Roman Britain, with the only exceptions being some rural sites that continued the Iron Age pattern. Most sites were rich in a full range of materials with plentiful iron, glass and pottery, and good quantities of copper alloys, lead, tin, silver and occasionally gold (**38**). The humble iron nail, for instance, is found in quantities not again seen until the Industrial Revolution.

Not only did the absolute numbers of objects increase but so did the range and levels of technology applied in their manufacture. The normal household objects typical of Iron Age sites were generally made using a low technology of craft manufacture. These were replaced by a technology that resulted from larger-scale and more specialized production techniques. Specialist workers now had access to equipment produced with investments of time and resources (see **66**). In the towns, small workshops used by specialist craftsmen betoken full-time employment in this work. Despite the much-increased volume of manufacture there is little evidence of major growth in the size of the productive units. We are left with the impression of an economy still based around small-scale craft

40 *(above)* Lead ingot found at Brough-on-Humber. It bears an inscription that reads in translation: 'Product of Gaius Julius Protus. British Lutudarensian lead from the lead-silver works.' It was produced in the Peak District and probably brought down the River Trent to Brough, a trans-shipment point for goods moving from inland rivers to the North Sea. Lead and silver were extracted in Britain from as early as AD 49 when bullion mining was under military control. Later production was handled by civilian contractors such as the man who owned the works that produced this ingot.

production. Where we do see a significant change is in the removal of any exclusive association between the best traditional craftsmen and the governing elite. There were new ways in which the powerful could show off their status, especially through the use of Roman architecture and domestic decoration, but the traditional classes of decorative metalwork manufacture no longer seem to have been under the sole control of tribal leaders. Rich objects from a wide range of sites imply the breakdown of this monopoly. The reasons for this are various. The control of precious metals moved to the imperial government immediately after the conquest (**40**) and gold and silver were also removed from circulation when captured as booty during the invasion. Likewise changes in taste and the fashions of wealth and status display were stimulated by the arrival of new things like Roman dress, architecture and sculpture.

These changes in manufacture were accompanied by increased distances over which many goods were transported to their consumers. While on Iron Age rural settlements the bulk of pottery and other goods was of local origin, on a similar Roman site equivalent goods had been produced over a far greater range of distances. There was thus a much wider variety of objects of specialized use and also a much higher volume of waste. In this sense wide areas of the Roman province were incorporated into a society where there was wide access to material wealth (**39**).

Developments in production were accompanied by a vast increase in the importation of goods from elsewhere in the empire. These traded commodities, which included Mediterranean foodstuffs such as olive oil as well as comparatively low-value objects such as decorated pottery, also achieved a wide distribution and are found on many different types of site (see **65**).

The processes that led to these changes are entwined with the Roman imperial system to which we now turn.

2 NATIVES AND THE ROMAN SYSTEM

The Roman imperial system was coercive, but relied heavily on building an identity of interest between Rome and the rulers of conquered territories. They could then be left to govern themselves on Rome's behalf without the need for an enormous central bureaucracy or army of occupation. This practice was born of necessity since Rome existed in a world of slow communication and was itself governed by a small elite.

By the time Britain was invaded, the Roman army and administration were increasingly peopled by natives from other provinces (**41**). They had adopted Roman cultural values and trappings and had normally obtained the legal status of Roman citizenship that brought with it both personal prestige and practical advantages. Personal advancement was obtained through service in the Roman army or in civil life. Much that we call 'Roman' was derived not from Rome itself but from a metropolitan mixture of Roman, Classical Greek and other European cultures. The artefacts and art illustrate this varied and hybrid character which permeated a vast area across Europe, the Middle East and North Africa. Britain thus came to share in a culture which although varied was unified by Romanized values, systems of organization and art styles.

The variety of styles within the Romanized areas cannot be taken as evidence that Britain was more superficially Roman than other provinces. The symbols of Romanization, the adoption of new styles and the speaking of Latin, were actively used to incorporate different peoples into the empire. This process of adopting new values, which we call Romanization, involved two-way contact between natives and Romans, so patterns varied according to the nature and history of both the native peoples and the Romans with whom they came into contact. As there were important differences between the various tribes even within Britain, let alone across the empire, the mosaic of cultures was highly variable yet unified by a common strand of Roman culture.

The ways in which the new culture was adopted in Britain also varied with particular circumstances. Some indigenous rulers wanted to appear Roman. Having suffered either defeat at the hands of the Roman army, or diplomatic coercion prior to a surrender, their own authority was compromised. Their social positions had previously been demonstrated with symbols of power such as warrior equipment and horse trappings, which showed their

41 *(below)* Tombstone of the procurator C. Julius Alpinus Classicianus, financial administrator of the province, who was brought in after the Boudiccan revolt of AD 60–1. He probably came from northern Gaul, and he is a good example of a provincial who rose to an important position within the Roman administration. In translation the inscription reads: 'To the spirits of the departed and of Gaius Julius Alpinus Classicianus (son of Gaius) ... Procurator of the Province of Britain. Julia Pacata Iniduta, his wife, had this built.'

ability to control their peoples. Roman control brought important changes that undermined these marks of status. The Romans discouraged the bearing of arms in public, and the incentives to parade military prowess were lessened. The rapid influx of an increased volume of Roman goods following the conquest made hitherto scarce objects more widely available. This reduced their rarity so that ownership no longer symbolized the highest prestige. Within a generation after the conquest native leaders were thus seeking new means of marking their social superiority.

Indigenous leaders were by now active participants in the Roman system and so they adopted symbols that identified them with the conquerors. This not only ingratiated them with their masters but also identified them with the new power structure in the eyes of their peoples. The adoption of Roman building styles in the new towns and in the countryside, plus the emergence of Roman art at this time, can be attributed to this process. Native use of Roman styles enabled the elites to maintain and enhance their individual status with both their new masters and their own people. The adoption of things Roman applied not only to material trappings. The new language, Latin, and new customs, like the wearing of Roman dress (the toga), also defined social standing.

The threat of Roman force was always present although rarely used to suppress native insurrection. The Boudiccan revolt of AD 60–1 reminds us that it could be used when tribal discontent erupted as a result of insensitive actions by the occupying forces. Immediately after the conquest of a native tribe, goods and territories confiscated were returned provided the tribe conducted themselves in accordance with Roman practice and aims. The defeated people lost their right to conduct wars or manage their own foreign affairs, and became subject to Roman taxation. Moreover they were expected to organize themselves according to Roman constitutional traditions under the supervision of the Roman governor. This man came from the upper ranks of Roman society and usually served in his province for only three years. In places native kingship did survive for a generation or so after the conquest where this suited Roman purposes. Thus the pro-Roman king Cogidubnus reigned in central-southern England down to the 70s. However, even these tribes were eventually organized according to a Roman-style constitution with magistrates replacing kings.

42 *(right)* Map showing the *civitates* into which Roman Britain was divided. These administrative districts were based on Roman understanding of the pre-Roman tribes. As such, they fossilized the geography of the province as at the time of the invasion.

The government of the provinces was modelled on the Mediterranean city-state. Power was held by those who owned property worth more than a sum set down in a town's constitution. Those with sufficient wealth formed the council and pairs of magistrates were elected annually from among their number. They ran the day-to-day affairs of the territory, which included the surrounding countryside as well as the central town. Town and country together made up the city-state or *civitas* (**42**). This form of organization did not exist in Britain before the conquest, but many conquered tribes were treated by the Roman administration as if they were city-states. This resulted from the Roman perception that the city-state was the universal political form into which native tribal organization fitted. An analogy is the way that the nineteenth-century European powers perceived the world in terms of nation states and therefore divided their own empires into units of government that they could treat in the same way. The treatment of the tribes of Britain as city-states perpetuated an organization that was partly artificial, and failed to exploit potential in other regions. The wartime confederacy of clans that formed the Brigantes was treated as a single *civitas,* although at the time of the conquest they were not a single centralized people. In contrast, areas like that occupied by the Catuvellauni in Hertfordshire contained several developed settlements, any of which might have been chosen as centres for a *civitas;* in the event only one, Verulamium, was selected.

This framework provided native leaders with opportunities for self-advancement. This was in the Roman interest, for their indulgence in political competition defused anti-Roman sentiment and encouraged their Roman aspirations. For the natives the best opportunities for gaining preferment lay in political involvement. Tribes were thus gradually converted into Roman-style units of local government without deliberate social engineering by the conquerors. This is not to say that efforts were not expended on encouraging the new provincials in Roman ways. One aim was to develop a provincial identity. In the Iron Age there had been no concept of Britain as a place, for each person belonged to an autonomous clan or tribe. By bringing the tribes together and organizing them into a Roman province, Rome thus created Britain.

In the mid-50s, work began on the construction of a temple dedicated to the deified emperor Claudius who had died in AD 54. It was built in a compound on the edge of the newly founded town at Colchester (**43**). This was a *colonia* populated by retired legionary soldiers, which had been founded in 49 on the site of a legionary fortress when the army moved forward into the Midlands. It lay on the site of the *oppidum,* called Camulodunon in Celtic, which was the principal native tribal centre of the southeast before the invasion (see **23**). The temple of Claudius was a massive Classical-style structure comparable with the provincial religious centres built at Lyon in Gaul and Tarragona in Spain during the first century AD. All were designed as centres for ceremonies and assemblies of representatives from the cities of their provinces. The foundation of the first *colonia* in Britain at Colchester and the construction of the temple point to the creation of such a focus for Britannia. It engendered a potent image and new ethos that associated the interests of the native elite with those of Rome.

The symbol widely used to encourage loyalty to Rome was the image of the emperor in the form of sculpture and on coins (see **92**). Before the era of mass communication a knowledge of the face of the person in power had a potency it lacks today, although the familiar portrait of the monarch in a government office continues the tradition. The identification of the ruler with a god gradually

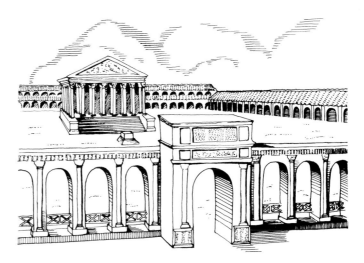

43 *(right)* The temple of the Deified Emperor Claudius built at Colchester between AD 54 and 60–1. The temple was the principal cult centre for the newly conquered province. It was constructed beside the new *colonia* and probably had a meeting-place for a council drawn from the different *civitates* of the province situated next to it. The Classical-style temple with the altar in front symbolized the new cultural order and Rome's subjugation of Britain.

became a commonplace throughout the Roman Empire. A number of dedications to the divine emperor, the spirit of the emperor or the divine imperial house illustrates their wide importance. A provincial identity was thus created and a common purpose established between the peoples of Britain and their conquerors.

While the leaders of indigenous society and those on the make often came to identify with Roman power, the surviving evidence is certainly biased towards them. Those who actively resisted, like Boudicca who led a major revolt of AD 60–1, were suppressed by the military might of Rome. Some who opposed Rome, like Venutius, fled beyond her reach, but those who resisted in other ways, whether passively or actively, are hardly represented in the surviving evidence.

URBANIZATION

The city-state or *civitas* included a rural territory administered from the central town. There were great variations across the empire between the towns used as administrative centres of these districts. Even within Britain differences can be identified. There were both geographical contrasts and divergences in form at different times. The towns can also be distinguished by the administrative status given them by Rome. Towns are normally divided into *coloniae, municipia* and *civitates,* each of which accorded different privileges of citizenship to their inhabitants.

Three of the British *coloniae* (Colchester, Lincoln and Gloucester) were built for those with Roman citizenship (legally, citizenship of the city of Rome itself). By the time of Britain's conquest this included men discharged from legionary service after completion of their term who had thereby earned a grant of land and citizenship. With time, other cities increasingly sought grants

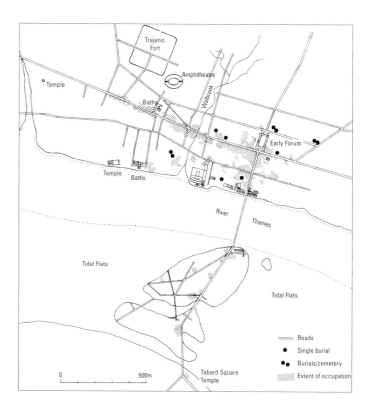

44 *(right)* Simplified plan of early Roman London. Settlements were established on either side of the river *c.* AD 50. That on the north bank was probably occupied by Roman citizens, many of whom migrated from other provinces. London was the centre of the road network and grew to become the largest town in the province. After the Boudiccan revolt of AD 60–1, it also became the centre of government for the province with the procurator, the governor and his military staff based there.

of colonial status as a matter of civic pride, and this was how York became a *colonia* at the beginning of the third century. It may have been provided while the emperor Septimius Severus and his entourage were staying there during his military campaigns in Scotland. Although it is sometimes claimed that London attained the same status during the middle years of Roman rule, there is no convincing evidence to support this plausible suggestion.

The second legal category was the *municipium,* a settlement that existed at the conquest, whose inhabitants had been allies of Rome and were thus recognized as a self-governing community with the grant of legal privileges. Those who had served as their magistrates were given Latin citizenship (notional membership of the tribes first conquered by Rome in the Italian region of Latium), a status favourable to the tribal aristocracy. The only certain *municipium* was Verulamium (near St Albans), the later Iron Age *oppidum* called 'Verlamion' in Celtic, which rapidly became a highly Romanized town from which the *civitas* of the Catuvellauni was governed. It gained its rank soon after the conquest, perhaps through co-operation during the invasion. As with the *coloniae, municipia* became more widespread across the empire as a result of promotion in the later

45 *(right)* Dedicatory inscription from the temple site at Tabard Square, Southwark, London. In translation it reads: 'To the divinities of the two emperors and to the god Mars Camulus, Tiberinius Celerianus, a citizen of the Bellovaci, seafarer of Londoners ... Primus ...' The man making the dedication comes from the *civitas* of the Bellovaci, whose territory lay in northern Gaul. Mars Camulus is a god generally associated with northern Gaul. The inscription provides evidence of London having been settled by a community of Gallic traders.

Roman period. Despite the claims made for some British towns, there is no evidence that any others were promoted to this status.

The final group are the *civitates peregrine* (towns of non-citizens), which included the bulk of Britain's administrative centres. There were probably legal distinctions between them depending upon the history of their incorporation by Rome. Such variations provided tax immunities for those that had supported Rome during annexation, but these cannot be identified with the available evidence. These three major categories included all but one of the major towns that were graced with suites of public administrative buildings and can be referred to as 'public towns'.

The single place that had such administrative buildings but does not fit into any of these classes is London (**44**), which was founded around AD 50. There is no evidence that it acted as the chief town of a *civitas,* so it is rather unusual in the Roman world. It probably began its existence as a trading centre, founded by immigrants from other provinces who came to take advantage of the commercial opportunities offered by the new province (**45**). The administrative buildings suggest that they organized themselves as an independent and self-governing community of Roman citizens. However,

46 *(right)* Map showing the principal roads, towns and legionary forts in Roman Britain.
A *Coloniae*
B *Civitas*-capitals and London
C Small towns
D Legionary forts occupied after the first century

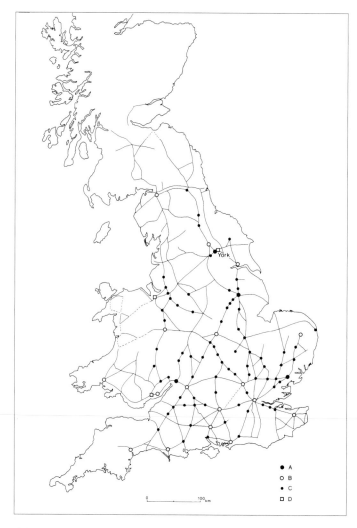

following the Boudiccan revolt of 60–1, which completely destroyed London, Colchester and Verulamium, the provincial administration seems to have transferred to London from Colchester. The province's financial administrator in the years immediately following the revolt was buried there (see **41**), and before the end of the first century the provincial governor was based here too. A fort in the northwest corner of the city housed the governor's guard and a staff drawn from other military units and deployed on administrative duties in London.

The whole province outside direct military control came within the territory of one of these cities (**46**). Their districts also contained a range of other settlements including towns. The legal status of these smaller urban sites, generally referred to as *vici,* made them

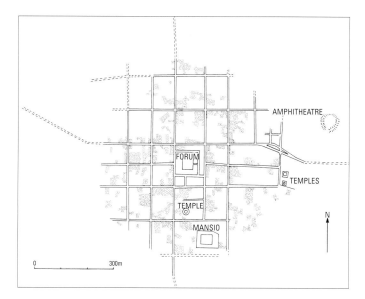

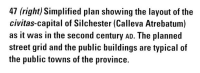

47 *(right)* Simplified plan showing the layout of the *civitas*-capital of Silchester (Calleva Atrebatum) as it was in the second century AD. The planned street grid and the public buildings are typical of the public towns of the province.

subservient to the *civitates,* although many acted as administrative centres of territorial subdivisions *(pagi).* Such districts perhaps perpetuated clan divisions derived from pre-conquest society. They were important especially where a *civitas* territory was extensive and difficult to govern from a single centre. Many *vici* also originated through the development of roadside settlements, which grew up to serve the imperial postal service (the *cursus publicus).* These were way-stations *(mutationes)* and inns *(mansiones)* where those on official business could change horses, eat and find accommodation, and were established at distances of about 25 km (16 miles) along the principal highways throughout the empire.

THE PUBLIC TOWNS

The administration role of these towns is evident in their planning and buildings, which set them apart from the small towns (**47, 48**). Their character was created by a combination of Roman official guidance and indigenous enterprise, so, although each city was different, all conformed to the same general pattern. All were planned around a grid of streets, the focus of which was invariably the principal public building, the forum/basilica (**49**). In Britain the forum was usually a square courtyard surrounded on three sides by a roofed veranda or portico, and on the fourth by the substantial hall of the basilica. This was a meeting-hall used as a law court and place where the town's official business was transacted. A small chamber used by the council was often attached, together with offices. The forum was in part a commercial focus but is better understood by

48 *(above)* Aerial photograph of part of Roman Silchester (47). Clearly visible are the lines of the streetgrid and buildings. The core area of city was surrounded by a defensive wall (also seen), probably built around the middle of the third century on the line of an earlier earthwork. The provision of urban defences seems to have been a display of urban status rather than a response to any military threat.

comparison with the Mediterranean town square of today: the centre of town life used for informal meetings between citizens, who gather to talk about the world, and to be seen. The vital central role of the forum was reinforced by the presence in it of statues and inscriptions that proclaimed the town's laws, history, pride and traditions (see **12**).

At the centre of the Roman world a city's public buildings were largely provided by rich individual citizens who became a town's benefactors. Those who competed for public office made gifts to the town to add to its splendour and enhance its standing in relation to the neighbouring cities. In Britain there is less evidence for this kind of munificence. Towns had few superfluous buildings and there are not many inscriptions proclaiming the generosity of individual benefactors. However, the principal towns were not without the facilities expected by a contemporary from elsewhere in the Roman world. They usually had a range of different temples, a set of public baths supplied with water piped from an aqueduct, and drained by a sewerage system, as well as places of entertainment, most commonly an amphitheatre but occasionally also a theatre. Although modest, these facilities provided for the basic needs of what was considered a civilized life. These public facilities began to be built soon after the conquest and most public towns had acquired a respectable range of facilities by the middle years of the second century. The architectural evidence shows that help with construction came from Gaul and Germany. The peoples of Britain had traditional contacts with these areas, and skills of stonemasonry and Roman building were established there by the time of Britain's development. The contacts that brought these crafts to Britain were probably fostered by Roman officials, some of whom originated in these areas. It was in their interests to give aid to the British communities as Rome did want to foster urbanism.

Many previous scholars have emphasized the role of the Roman army in the building of towns and the spreading of Roman architectural technology to the native peoples. However, studies of

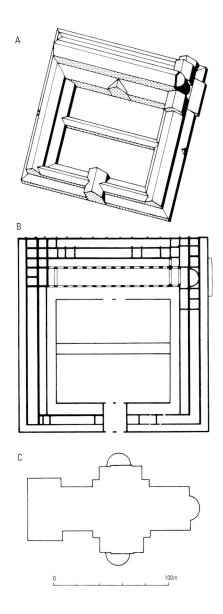

architectural details have shown that legionary stonemasons had little impact on the styles used in the emergent towns, most probably because they were too heavily involved in conquest, pacification and their own building work to be of direct assistance to the natives at the time when help was needed. There is also little archaeological support for the idea that public towns grew up as the result of the economic stimulus of the army or from settlements that had begun around the gates of temporary forts. Many towns, particularly in the south and east, grew up close to earlier native centres, often *oppida*. This suggests some continuity in the urban pattern, little affected by the army. Where this was not the case, principally in the north and west, military sites did influence urban development, although not through towns replacing settlements created by camp-followers. Instead, on their abandonment some fort sites were handed over to communities to form new towns. These forts already had planned layouts and standing buildings suitable for temporary adaptation to civil use. Such action undoubtedly helped the native peoples to develop an urban infrastructure and was thus a major contribution to the development of the province.

The substantial money invested in town building also raises questions about society. Although the Iron Age peoples had significant wealth, it was not necessarily in the form of cash needed to pay for building projects. Moreover the spending of money from the imperial treasury on such facilities for individual cities was not normal. Cash for such projects could have been generated in several ways, each of which has interesting implications. The circulation of coinage stimulated growth in trade and enabled those with commodities needed in the towns to make money. Those most able to benefit from the boom were probably people who produced saleable products. This included landowners who were also at the centre of politics in the emergent towns. Anyone, either a local or from abroad, who was able to build and rent out properties within the new towns could also have rapidly accumulated capital. The towns themselves probably also benefited from economic growth as they were entitled to levy local taxes in addition to those collected on behalf of the imperial treasury. The scale of these taxes was limited by the imperial authorities, but it may have been sufficient to help fund the maintenance of the towns.

The construction of the infrastructure needed for this economic growth could not have been provided without access to cash first.

49 *(above)* The forum and basilica of Roman London as it was in the early second century AD. This was the principal suite of buildings in the town and acted as both the administrative and the social focus for the community. One of the largest buildings in the western empire, it appears to have been too large for the community to support and later fell into decay.
A Suggested reconstruction
B Plan
C Outline plan of St Paul's Cathedral for comparison

Some wealthy Roman citizens (notably Seneca in the reign of Nero – 54–68) made large loans to the peoples of Britain with the aim of earning interest from the development of the province. Seneca's loan was enormous, the equivalent of 10,000 pounds of gold – enough to pay nearly nine legions for a year. As the lenders expected a financial return on their investments, economic growth in Britain must have been anticipated. Seneca recalled his loans, however, possibly suggesting that the profits did not fulfil initial expectations. A perhaps more stable source of money was the government itself, for, while direct grants from emperors to cities were unusual, Rome did sometimes allow a municipality to retain tax revenues collected on its behalf to spend on a civic project. Such dispensations, made on the advice of the governor, may have been treated as a form of political patronage. Although limited in duration, they provided opportunities for cities to spend significant sums on urban development. These two methods may have been in Tacitus' mind when he wrote that the governor Agricola gave 'private encouragement and official assistance' in the development of the towns in the late 70s.

The pattern of private buildings changed through time. In the earliest phases areas between the public buildings were crowded with unpretentious domestic buildings of modest size (see **21**). They were typically rectangular timber structures in which domestic and commercial activities coexisted. Street frontages were occupied by shops or workshops while living-quarters were towards the back and presumably also on upper floors. These buildings were the living- and working-places of those who made the towns vibrant economic centres within the rapidly developing province. However, within these towns during the first and second centuries it is difficult to identify the houses of obviously rich people who held political power. It may be that, as in the Iron Age, there was very little distinction between the houses of people of different rank.

During the second and third centuries larger and more elaborate town houses appeared (**50**). These were almost certainly occupied by an urban elite, and by the fourth century the towns were dominated by stone-built mansions that were manifestly their residences. The problem in understanding the nature of the later towns is not in identifying the houses of the rich, but rather in locating the whereabouts of the urban proletariat upon whose production urban prosperity was based. In contrast to the towns two centuries earlier,

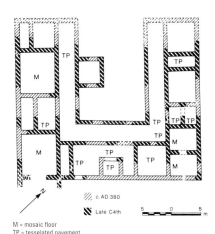

M = mosaic floor
TP = tesselated pavement

50 *(above)* Plan of a late-Roman town house in Insula 27 at Verulamium (St Albans). The public towns of the later Roman period came to be dominated by large houses in contrast to the more functional timber buildings of earlier centuries (**21**), suggesting a move towards luxury residence rather than commerce.

there was an absence of small and unpretentious shops and workshops. These fourth-century cities also show a decline in their public facilities. Many of the major buildings constructed earlier were left to decay or were demolished. Even where this did not occur, there is little evidence that facilities were properly maintained or extended, as might be expected if they had continued to be of key importance.

These changes in internal organization coincided with alterations to their external appearances created by the enclosure of the towns within walls, especially during the later second and third centuries (see **48**). This contrasts with the normal pattern in the western Roman Empire where during the *pax Romana* towns generally had no defences. The Roman government discouraged their construction both to prevent any possible internal security risk and to discourage over-extravagant civic building projects.

Urban enclosure began in the mid-first century when a small group of the towns of southern Britain was provided with earthwork defences. These centres all had a legal status that technically left them outside the governor's jurisdiction, so they were free to act as they wished in this matter. Their defences were probably constructed in the tradition of displaying status through the erection of dykes, as around *oppida,* hill-forts and farmsteads during the Iron Age.

The main period of building urban enclosures was in the latter part of the second century and has sometimes been associated with the removal of troops by the governor Clodius Albinus, in his attempt to wrest power from Septimius Severus in 193. This is neither plausible nor necessary. The defences took time to construct and are unlikely to have been built over such a short period. Equally there is no evidence to suggest any concerted defensive strategy. Most evidence points to the construction of town defences at the initiative of local communities and not as a result of a central command. The earthen banks of the second and third centuries were often graced with more elaborate stone gateways on the principal approaches. Subsequently stone walls were constructed to replace many of the earthworks and some were finally elaborated with the addition of external towers around the most visible lengths of the walls. The considerable investment of resources in the construction and development of defences thus became a symbol of civic aspirations, despite the fact that within the towns little was found to impress visitors from outside the province.

The size range of Roman towns is considerable. London, the largest centre, had a total area (including the Southwark suburb) of around 160 ha (395 acres) with a population of perhaps 30,000. This is twice the size of the next largest city, Cirencester, and more than ten times that of the average small town. The majority of the public towns had a size of about 40 ha (99 acres), and hence a population of perhaps 6–7,000 people. These estimates make clear that the scale of urbanism in Roman Britain was modest.

Their modest size does not detract from their social significance. People who moved to the towns came from close-knit rural communities, so the growth of urban populations led to the emergence of a society partially dislocated from its roots in tribal and family networks. By breaking away from the bonds of traditional society those in the towns had obtained social mobility and were freer to exploit new opportunities. The towns provide evidence for the increasing social differentiation. The major beneficiaries of the Roman system became wealthy through trading outside the constraints of tribal control and gained prestige by embracing Roman culture. The less successful lacked the support of clan and family and perhaps fell into poverty and distress in ways prevented by the support networks of a tribal society. Towns thus became places where traditional society was broken down and a new order established; within them we see an increasing differentiation between the haves and the have-nots.

Even the largest towns remained on a human scale: agricultural activities and even farms permeated all of them. The inappropriateness of the colossal early Imperial public buildings in these towns comes into focus, even though they were designed to serve large rural hinterlands. We can only really compare them with the cathedrals of the equally small medieval towns that similarly had a constant battle to construct and maintain their fabrics. The building of such public monuments was an emphatic statement of the aspirations of Romano-British society and emphasizes how influential Roman culture became in them.

THE SMALL TOWNS

These settlements had no primary role as administrative centres, were diverse in character and fulfilled a range of different functions. There is little general agreement about their definition, and the

51 *(right)* Aerial photograph showing the small town at Water Newton (Durobrivae) near Peterborough. In contrast to public towns such as Silchester (47), small towns rarely had rectangularly planned street layouts or major public buildings. Here we can see the principal Roman road running straight through the settlement with a network of irregular back streets on either side of it. A defensive wall, probably built during the second century, surrounds the settlement. As in other small towns, there were no major public buildings at the centre of the settlement.

smallest may simply have been agricultural villages. The *vici* that developed outside fort gates in frontier areas perhaps served the same functions as the small towns in civilian areas (see **62**). If we exclude those places that are primarily religious and thus best treated as sanctuaries, there remain 60–70 sites that arguably served as important local economic and social centres. Their density of distribution illustrates the need for the services they provided.

Most were smaller than the public towns, covering an average of about 5 ha (12 acres), although some of the largest rise above 10 ha (25 acres) in extent. Their populations were usually less than 1000, and may often have been considerably smaller. They lacked networks of gridded streets, being ribbon developments sprawled along the principal roads (**51**). Where nucleated, they were characterized by irregular lanes that resulted from gradual organic growth. The majority contained a relatively low density of buildings, many of which were simple, functional, rectangular houses with workshops or shops under the same roof. There were rarely any substantial town houses, and the general absence of major public buildings is also notable. Where these did occur, they are usually inns *(mansiones)* built to serve the imperial post, and were most often located near the limits of settlements. The impression is of modest towns or villages which served the day-to-day needs of the agricultural population and lacked the pretensions of the Romanized administrative centres.

The origins, growth and functions of the small towns are matters of considerable debate although some patterns are now clearly established. There were clear regional distinctions. In the south and east most grew up at or near Iron Age nucleated settlements, although those located on the Roman road network thrived while those less favourably positioned often declined. New centres also grew up in this region, especially around the inns constructed for the imperial postal service on roads. In the north and west, Iron Age settlement nucleation was less common and the growth of small towns was more often related to military activities. Some started as civilian settlements outside the gates of the forts and continued as independent settlements when the army moved forward.

Settlement growth, stimulated by opportunities for providing services to a cash-rich military population, was important in areas where forts were long established, as witnessed by the growth of *vici* outside frontier forts. However, short-lived military occupation had less of a permanent effect. In these areas the forts' prime importance was in refocusing the geography. Forts were constructed at strategic points and new roads built to connect them. Both forts and roads defined a new and dominant geographical framework that has often endured into our present landscape. The local population was drawn towards the fort, which became the natural centre of the landscape even after the military had moved on. Where there were native Iron Age centres the Roman forts were generally positioned to oversee them, and road networks were thus determined by the existing political geography.

In addition to settlements that grew up to fulfil the day-to-day needs of the population, several towns emerged as centres for particular economic activities. Lead and silver production at Charterhouse in the Mendips and ironworking at Weston-under-Penyard in the Forest of Dean are significant examples. Elsewhere the salt industry is associated with the growth of Droitwich, and several towns, most notably Water Newton, were closely associated with the large-scale manufacture of pottery. In all these towns economic prosperity owed something to industrial specialization, although all were also important regional centres for agricultural production and day-to-day trading.

The success of the largest minor towns is of particular interest since throughout their histories they remained as vibrant economic centres that contrast with the public towns which became increasingly dominated by substantial houses rather than artisan dwellings. This illustrates a fundamental distinction between the two types of town. The small towns were a barometer for the economic life of the province while the public towns were the focus of political life and the administration.

52 *(above)* Aerial photograph of the Roman villa at Ditchley, Oxon. The photograph shows the principal residence, surrounded by an enclosure ditch and wall. Partially visible to the front of the courtyard are the walls of subsidiary buildings. The elements of planned layout and symmetry are clearly seen. Modest villas such as this were characteristic of later Roman Britain but probably represented the homes of only about one per cent of the rural population.

RURAL SETTLEMENT

There was an inextricable link between land ownership and political power in the Roman world since those aspiring to municipal office had to fulfil a wealth qualification measured in terms of land ownership. This placed a particular premium on the control of rural estates and had a fundamental effect on the pattern of rural settlement. Southern Britain also adopted the Roman tradition whereby those in political power exhibited their status through building substantial rural houses that we call villas. Although most of the countryside remained dominated by unpretentious farmsteads, most archaeological attention has been paid to these villas which number about 1000 and were inhabited by no more than 1 per cent of the rural population. As a result we have a reasonable picture of their distribution and development.

Before looking at these patterns we should clarify the meaning of the term 'villa' as its use by archaeologists is often confused. Villas were distinguished from other rural buildings by the use of Roman architectural styles and decoration (**52**). Indigenous roundhouses and simple rectangular timber structures were replaced by more complex arrays of interconnected rectangular rooms which were given an external architectural unity by the addition of a façade or portico, designed to provide an impression of classicism. The key lies not in the achievement of a purely Classical architectural form but in their aspiration towards Roman style. Structures that reveal attempts to appear Roman can thus be distinguished from those that remained wholly native in their inspiration. They also show expenditure on a particular form of display. Most villas were built on land farmed by their proprietors although this means neither that they all were primarily farms, nor that the money spent on their construction was drawn principally from farming the land on which they stood. Villas represent expenditure of wealth, not evidence of how it was produced. Even where farming was associated with particular villas it need not have generated the money that supported the villa's occupants.

Villa development began soon after the conquest of the south and east in the traditional heartlands of developed Iron Age culture. These early villas were bold and magnificent proclamations of the new order and certainly not modest structures. The most

53 *(above* Reconstructed view of the villa at Fishbourne, West Sussex, as it probably appeared around the end of the first century AD. This building was among the finest in Britain and shows how existing wealth was invested in new, Romanized forms of display in the years after the conquest.

impressive was located at Fishbourne near Chichester, within the boundaries of the Iron Age *oppidum* and on the site of an invasion-period military base. Its earliest phases were impressive, but discreet when contrasted with the gigantic Mediterranean-style mansion completed within about thirty years of the invasion (**53**). It has been plausibly suggested that its owner was the British king Cogidubnus who ruled this part of the country on behalf of Rome until the time of the Emperor Vespasian (AD 69–79). Ownership by a native aristocrat would be consistent with the pattern at other early British villas that succeeded native farmsteads on the same sites. Such topographical continuity suggests a continued ownership and its repetition at a number of sites leads us to conclude that native leaders adopted the Roman ideal of owning splendid rural houses in order to express their identification with Roman culture.

The earliest villas are larger than average. Not all were as enormous as Fishbourne, but few were of the tiny size that characterized many during the third and fourth centuries. These early villas did not evolve slowly as their owners gradually accumulated the money to invest in enlarging and aggrandizing their rural houses. Instead they resulted from the investment of extant capital in this new form of status display, strongly suggesting that they were built by and for the native aristocracy who wished to embrace new Roman values. Villa building also implies permanence, which marks an important break from the Iron Age tradition of building in timber. The use of durable stone perhaps symbolized a security in the control of political power that had not previously existed. While Iron Age farmsteads were often rebuilt on the same spot within long-lived enclosures, houses seem to have been replaced each generation. Although land was a saleable commodity under the new regime, the idea of spending wealth on

54 *(right)* Map showing the overall distribution of villas in Roman Britain. The pattern shows a concentration in the regions where civilian administration within the *civitates* became most strongly established. It was in these areas that native aristocrats adopted Roman ways of life, including living in sometimes-opulent rural villas.

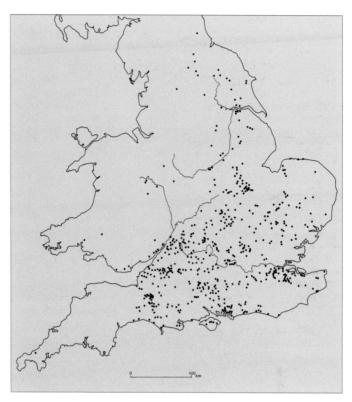

immovable bricks and mortar, rather than keeping it in a form with which one could flee, illustrates a significant social change.

From the later first century onwards there were changes in the pattern of villa growth and distribution, which saw their establishment over a broader region of southern Britain. At the peak of their numbers and distribution in the early fourth century they were found over the whole of lowland Britain, with the most northerly examples in County Durham, and other outliers in Cornwall and Wales (**54**). They not only spread geographically but also down the social pyramid, for as their numbers increased so their average size decreased. The desire to build in a Roman style had thus spread, albeit to a still limited sector, through rural society.

Simple villa structures occur both as independent units and in combinations that formed the larger villas characteristic of the later Roman period. In these a number of buildings were deployed around an open courtyard often in a rather ramshackle layout, suggesting that they had not been planned as a unity, but had grown gradually as wealth was accumulated and spent on building. Architectural unity was provided by the addition of corridors and porticoes designed to hide the disparate buildings behind a façade

55 *(right)* Reconstruction drawing showing the villa at Gadebridge Park, Hertfordshire, as it probably appeared *c.* AD 325. The gradual evolution of the house led to an asymmetrical plan that was disguised from view behind a unifying façade.

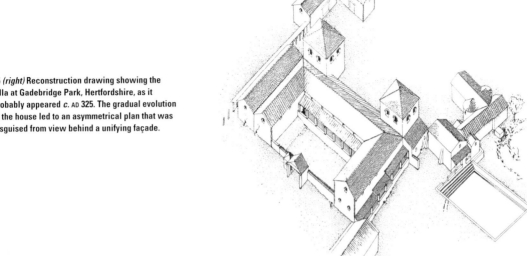

of unified style (**55**). The largest late Roman villas often had the richest decoration, in particular floor mosaics (**57**). There is no doubt that their layout and decoration was designed to overawe visitors and social inferiors.

An important aspect of villas was their relationship with the major towns around which many were clustered. At first sight this is simply explained as the result of the economic opportunities urban markets offered to agricultural producers. This economic link between agricultural producers and urban populations is indisputable, but its strength seems insufficient to explain the pattern. Some of the largest towns, like London, had remarkably small concentrations of villas around them, while much smaller centres, like Ilchester, were surrounded by large clusters. An analysis of their distributions has, however, shown that public towns were usually more significant magnets than small towns and their effect on the countryside spread over a larger area. Landowners engaged in politics in the public towns had an incentive to live in style as close as possible to their town. This enhanced the attractions of the towns as they became places where worthwhile social contacts could be made. The absence of similar opportunities at small towns left them as less attractive centres. However, while the villas were most common in the later Roman period, the public towns had their heyday at an earlier date, so the connection between their distributions may result simply from increased country living among those families who had concentrated on town life in previous generations. Such increased aristocratic interest in the countryside also became evident in the development of agriculture.

The scale of the largest villas makes it unlikely that they were inhabited solely by a single family. Even the extended family groups typical of Iron Age Britain would have been too small for the largest establishments. Many were built up of multiple units implying occupation by several separate groups. These may have been lived in by extended families or independent households of social clients clustered together to form the villa. The difficulty does not lie in making this observation, but in understanding it. The idea that it resulted from the Celtic legal system is unsatisfactory. If land was divided equally between heirs through the generations as in the system of partible inheritance, the result would have been a fragmentation of property holdings and the presence of large villas is at variance with this.

The clustering of buildings to form larger villas probably resulted from the accumulation of wealth and power by individuals. The houses of these magnates became the focus for communities of their retinues of dependants. These clients, retainers and workers lived in a range of different structures appropriate to their social rank and the group's organization. This pattern is perhaps a development of that seen in some Iron Age villages. However, in the villas architecture was used to distinguish between the houses of people of different status.

We have so far concentrated on the elite sites. Other settlements were very varied and we also find a wide range of agricultural features such as tracks and fields in the landscape. Many ordinary farmsteads, especially in the more remote areas, continued in occupation from the Iron Age without immediate or perceptible alterations in layout. Even these received small numbers of Roman objects indicating some participation in the new style of life. Often there were subtle changes in these farmsteads, such as enclosure ditches going out of use as the volume of imported objects increased.

In addition to these settlements a range of new forms emerged. Some resulted from the countryside becoming more cosmopolitan, as with the growth of major rural sanctuaries and smaller temples surrounded by facilities for visitors (**56**). These became economic as well as religious foci since temples almost certainly owned land and acted as estate centres like the great medieval monasteries. They

56 *(below)* Plan of the rural religious sanctuary at Nettleton, Wiltshire. The octagonal shrine dates to the later third century and was the focus of a small settlement that probably served pilgrims and housed those who farmed the surrounding land. Pagan temples owned estates, so the settlement also may have been occupied by the temple's own tenants.

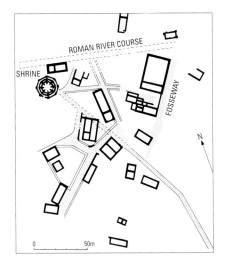

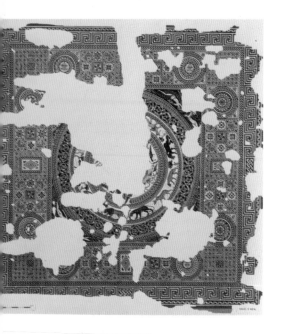

57 *(above)* Coloured drawing of the fourth-century mosaic pavement from the villa at Woodchester, Gloucestershire. This is the largest example known from Britain, measuring 14.9 m by 14.9 m (49 ft by 49 ft) and shows the development of the abstract geometrical patterns characteristic of British pavements. Around the central medallion, which once contained an image of Orpheus, are wild animals, a theme typical of great villas across the whole empire (drawn by David S. Neal).

therefore became places of agricultural production and minor craft activity associated with the estate. They also provided services for pilgrims who visited periodically or gathered for seasonal festivals accompanied by great fairs.

Similar villages emerged across much of lowland Britain during the later Roman period (**58**). Our knowledge of them is limited as they have not been the subject of very intensive study. In the fenland of East Anglia, which was progressively colonized by farmers from the later Iron Age onwards, we see the growth of a range of larger settlements, reaching a peak in the third century. Later the middle-sized sites disappeared, leaving small hamlets with up to four houses at one extreme and larger villages of up to ten at the other. Gradual population growth resulted in villages growing and surviving because they were well adapted to the vicissitudes of agricultural life. Population growth may also account for the emergence of villages elsewhere, but this does not seem a sufficient explanation in areas like the Cotswolds where some villages were considerably larger and show no evidence of gradual growth. These settlements were a characteristic of the fourth century, and some were sited close to some medium-sized villas. Like the houses in the small towns, those in villages were dwellings that also served as workshops. The impression is that these late Roman villages were a symbol of increasing class differentiation.

Classical sources refer to the emergence of semi-feudal tied peasants *(coloni)* in the late Roman period. These villages may have housed this dependent class, reliant on large landowners for at least part of their living. No fully feudal system developed, although as peasants gravitated towards nucleated settlements they became less independent than their ancestors. At some villages small fields behind the houseplots imply a crofter economy in which the inhabitants cultivated their own land as well as undertaking work for the landowner, whether as an obligation or for a wage. Elsewhere independent farmsteads and smaller villas continued to be occupied, so later Romano-British society was not simply divided into two classes. Instead, the pyramid of class differentiation had expanded so that a small wealthy minority dominated increasing numbers of dependants.

These social changes coincided with a period of agricultural innovation. The third and fourth centuries witnessed various changes

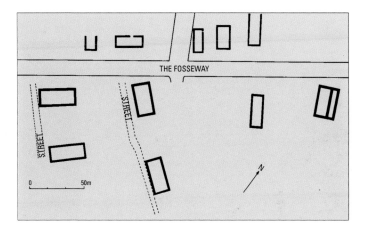

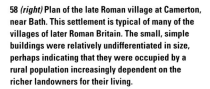

58 *(right)* Plan of the late Roman village at Camerton, near Bath. This settlement is typical of many of the villages of later Roman Britain. The small, simple buildings were relatively undifferentiated in size, perhaps indicating that they were occupied by a rural population increasingly dependent on the richer landowners for their living.

in the ways in which fields were ploughed, and crops harvested and processed. These developments included the introduction of a heavier plough that turned the soil over rather than just stirring it as with the earlier simple ard or scratch plough. This technology made deeper loamy soils more usable for arable agriculture. The first full use of crop-rotation systems also occurred, and both the balanced sickle and long scythe (for cutting grain and hay respectively) were introduced. Crop processing was also altered by both the introduction of the threshing sledge (which was used to free the grain from the ear) and an increased use of corn-drying ovens. These were probably used for several functions including malting as well as crop drying. In combination these innovations are evidence of significant changes in agricultural organization as they involved the use of both new technology and investment in new equipment.

Peasant farmers are traditionally conservative because they have neither the spare capital to expend on unknown and untried equipment nor the spare capacity to take risks with their livelihood. Later Roman innovation was thus more likely introduced by the aristocracy who were increasingly resident at their now more lavish villas. Their increased presence in the countryside may have encouraged experimentation and the introduction of a range of new technologies, which enabled a wider range of crop production from different qualities of land. As with the similar process in eighteenth-century England, this presumably increased the financial return from the land. This aristocratic presence in the countryside may also account for the increased evidence of hunting, which is shown by animal bones found in late Roman domestic rubbish deposits. Hunting was probably enjoyed as an elite pursuit, although the preference seems to have been for the edible deer and boar rather than the inedible fox.

3 ROMAN AUTHORITY AND ITS DEMANDS

CIVIL ADMINISTRATION

Roman provincial administration was applied to Britain by dividing the province into separate *civitas* territories, each centred on a public town and governed by an oligarchy drawn from the native aristocracy (see **42**). This essentially federal structure was overlain by a layer of Roman administration designed to oversee the cities and ensure that Roman interests remained paramount. There was no professional civil service in the early empire, so provincial government was run by a combination of different groups. The most senior office holders served periods as administrators in the provinces at stages in their careers within the political system of Rome itself. They progressed through a succession of posts, which gave them military and administrative experience in both Rome and the provinces so those who reached the pinnacle had a broadly based understanding. More minor officials were seconded to the civil administration from the ranks of the army.

The emperor's power was an effective fusion of the different strands of traditional authority. He was *imperator,* military commander-in-chief, but in theory relied for his constitutional power on the authority of the Senate. From time to time they appointed him as a consul, one of the chief magistrates, and also granted him the powers to govern as a tribune with authority over the Senate and magistrates. He was also chief priest and frequently proclaimed as father of the country. His office thus combined power in the military, civil and spiritual spheres.

As the emperor's control of the army ultimately underscored his power, provinces like Britain with a substantial army garrison were kept under his direct control rather than under the notional authority of the Senate. In these provinces governors were therefore appointed as personal representatives of the emperor from among those whom he could trust. Their responsibility was great as Britain's governor commanded one of the largest armies in the empire. He also needed to be loyal and might contribute to the emperor's prestige through his military success. Governors of Britain were initially drawn from among those who had been consuls at Rome and were at the apex of the political hierarchy. To have been elected and received preferment through their careers they had developed skills of political manipulation and held sufficient wealth to maintain strong political influence.

A characteristic of the early centuries of the empire was that power remained personal rather than institutional. The governor was the emperor's personal representative, whose duties were wide ranging. He commanded the army and led troops in the field when the emperor was absent. Slow communications meant that governors were directly responsible for both the strategy and the tactics of a campaign. The careers of first-century governors thus show that men were selected for their particular military expertise. The governor also dealt with a range of other matters, from military recruitment to diplomatic relations. When not engaged in military affairs, he was responsible for overseeing the government of the cities and acting as the ultimate judicial authority within his province. In dealings with the municipalities, government was generally reactive, with the governor responding to requests from towns' magistrates. During the middle years of the empire governors increasingly became responsible for preventing towns from indulging in unnecessarily extravagant expenditure that threatened communities' abilities to pay their taxes to Rome.

The major part of a governor's duties were judicial as he was responsible for any legal case involving a Roman citizen and for more serious offences concerning non-citizens. He travelled a circuit around his province, hearing cases in person. He also had jurisdiction in civil law where there were evidently problems in reconciling Celtic practices with Roman law. The governor and his staff were based in London from the later first century although for much of the year a governor would have toured his province. His household was composed of clients and friends who offered help and support while at the same time advancing their own careers. This unofficial group were vital to the success of his tour of duty, although they remained unpaid. At a lower level were the headquarters' staff of seconded soldiers, bureaucrats, clerical officers and messengers plus an escort for the governor and guards for prisoners.

Financial administration was not in the governor's hands but instead in the control of the procurator (see **41**). He was directly answerable to the emperor for both the collection of revenues and the payment of dues. This division of duties acted as a check on both office holders. Procurators were drawn from the equestrian order that held a rather ill-defined intermediate rank between senators and the ordinary citizens, but were important in serving as military and civil officials.

Members of the procurator's staff supervised the mines and acted as bailiffs for land owned by the emperor as well as dealing with the taxes that they themselves collected and those raised for Rome by the cities. They were also responsible for expenditure, with the principal outgoings being soldiers' salaries, which required liaison with Rome over the supply of coinage. As the scale and complexity of the province grew so did the number of minor officials in the procurator's department. It was these officials with whom provincials had most day-to-day contact.

Throughout the history of the empire, the scale of bureaucracy increased. This was brought about in particular by the subdivision of provinces into smaller administrative units. Around AD 197 Britain was divided into two: Britannia Superior (the province nearer to Rome) governed from London, and Britannia Inferior with its capital at York. This was designed to reduce the number of soldiers under the control of any one governor and was a consequence of the governor Clodius Albinus' attempt to gain imperial power by challenging Septimius Severus. This division naturally increased the scale of bureaucracy, and a similar effect resulted from a further subdivision into four at the end of the third century. Superior was subdivided into Britannia Prima (probably ruled from Cirencester) and Maxima Caesariensis (whose capital remained in London). York also retained its status as a capital, as the centre of Britannia Secunda, while the other half of its former province, now called Flavia Caesariensis, was administered from Lincoln.

The proliferation of smaller provinces reduced the status of governors at the same time as a new tier of administration was superimposed. The British provinces were subsumed within an overarching structure (the Gallic Praefecture), which was subdivided into a series of lesser administrative units or dioceses, each controlled by a *vicarius*. Britain formed a single diocese, probably governed from London, which thus retained its status as Britain's principal administrative centre. A greater number of officials became increasingly involved in the day-to-day running of affairs, and cities became less important and less attractive as routes to power for native aristocrats.

59 *(right)* Aerial photograph showing the Roman auxiliary fort at Hayton, East Yorkshire. The outline of the playing-card shape of the fort enclosure is clearly visible, together with an annexe that continues beneath the houses to the right of the fort in the picture. Excavation has demonstrated that this was a short-lived fort, occupied perhaps for a decade in the period shortly after AD 70, and was located here to oversee the local population during the period immediately following the Roman conquest of the area.

Soon after the conquest people from the more important provincial families began to acquire Roman citizenship. It was a reward for routine service or for special loyalty, as in the case of the client king Cogidubnus who was granted citizenship by Claudius. On acquiring citizenship provincials changed their names, often adopting the family name of their sponsor. The pattern of the personal names of citizens shows a peak in grants of citizenship in the middle of the first century, then only a trickle until the later second century.

Families who obtained citizenship rose through the ranks of the administration, although advancement generally took several generations. From the second century onwards emperors like Septimius Severus were drawn from the older-established Mediterranean provinces. Middle-ranking officials serving in Britain were increasingly drawn from provincial families, as in the case of Cn. Pompeius Homullus, procurator in the 90s, whose family was from Spain. In comparison with older-established provinces there is less evidence for participation by Britons in the imperial administration. This may be a result of her late addition to the empire or the comparatively small number of powerful families in each of the *civitates*. The integration of native aristocrats had the longer-term effect of creating a commonality of interest between those of equivalent social rank in different provinces, which gradually broke down the boundaries between the different peoples. This was enhanced by the movement of people between provinces that characterized life in the empire. Roman power thus reinforced distinctions between social classes rather than ethnic groups. This enabled people like the British monk Pelagius to move freely and contribute to intellectual debate in Rome from the 380s until he moved to Sicily and North Africa in 409.

Administrative jobs gave access to a power structure that rose above the increasingly limited prospects available in the cities. Municipal posts were less politically powerful and had become burdensome. The costs of contributing to the running of towns and the 'voluntary' contributions expected from civic officials were heavier, not least because there were fewer willing to shoulder them. Thus successive later Roman laws obliged those eligible to serve as magistrates. As state servants were exempted from compulsory municipal service and taxation there was an added attraction to a career outside the local sphere.

THE ARMY

Although the army was heavily involved in campaigning, it was more often a static force based in its forts on and behind the frontiers. The army was of unquestioned benefit to the State when the empire was expanding with the acquisition of new territory and wealth. However, as expansion slowed and the army became static, it became not only a drain on resources but also an increasingly destabilizing influence. The imperial succession was secured as often by force of arms as by constitutional means, so control of the army was crucial. Success in war gave the emperor military kudos, and there always remained the unconquered and periodically troublesome northern tribes to be attacked. The history of Roman Britain is punctuated by vague hints of 'troubles' quashed by campaigns, often at the stage when a new emperor was establishing himself.

The distribution of the army in Britain evolved through three principal phases. In the first century its positioning was a response to the geography of the tribal territories encountered. In the areas where there were developed Iron Age nucleated sites, auxiliary forts were positioned to oversee native centres of power and to control strategic routes (**59**). The legionary forts were situated as a strategic reserve, either behind a region just captured or looking forward, at the next tribe to face conquest.

From the end of the first century, the military were regrouped to form an increasingly ordered frontier (see **7**). This remained forward-looking, but a frontier was eventually fixed on the line of Hadrian's Wall (see **27–29**). This was a linear barrier, with a complex and slowly evolved architecture, designed to control movement into and out of the province by channelling it through a limited number of gateways. As such it was not a line designed to be defended but provided a security barrier for the province with permanent bases along it.

In the final phase of military strategy the total size of the garrison declined significantly and the distribution changed from one designed for an offensive strategy to one organized for defence. Although Hadrian's Wall and the hinterland forts in the north and throughout Wales continued in use, their garrison sizes were reduced and the troops were of second-rate status, classified as *limitanei* – permanently stationed frontiersmen. These borders remained largely peaceful and secure and so did not demand particular attention from the Roman authorities. Increasing emphasis was placed on the construction of new-style forts around the coast, particularly in southern and eastern England (**60, 61**). These had high walls and secure gates that made them more readily defensible, rather like medieval castles. They were clearly designed as strong-points to be held against the marauding barbarians who had attacked other parts of the western empire during the third century. Their particular concentration around the southern and eastern coasts reflects the perception of an increased threat from across the North Sea (see **10**).

Another strategic change seen in the late Roman army was the increased emphasis upon the use of mobile rapid-deployment forces under the command of a *comes,* or count. His troops (the *comitatenses)* were the crack forces, but are hardly attested in Britain, presumably because the province was neither particularly important nor under as much threat from insurgents as other regions. The absence of these troops was probably beneficial to the province since the mobile army was billeted on the provincials and the arrival of one's own troops could be as destructive as a raid by the enemy. The decline in the manning levels on the frontier and the absence of a mobile field army meant that the total army size in fourth-century Britain declined to perhaps somewhere between 10,000 and 20,000.

Assessing the impact of the army on the civilian population starts from the realization that soldiers were always unevenly distributed across the country. Areas rapidly incorporated into the empire were not long affected by the military. Where the army

60 *(above)* Aerial shot of the fort at Richborough, Kent. In the centre of the fort the cross-shaped foundation is the base of a four-way monumental arch, built towards the end of the first century AD. Surrounding this is a square enclosure constructed in the early third century, forming a military stronghold around the by-then ruined arch that was probably used as a look-out tower. The final major phase of defensive architecture is the tall flint-built wall of the Saxon Shore fort enclosing the whole site, built *c.* AD 275.

61 *(below)* The late third-century walls of the Saxon Shore fort at Burgh Castle, Suffolk. Tall walls with external towers characterize military defences of the later Roman period and illustrate a change in tactics towards defence.

remained stationed its presence was much more influential. The imposition of a military base involved the requisition of native lands for both the fort and the territory needed to feed and exercise the soldiers' animals. The imposition of military rule also robbed local native leaders of opportunities to participate in local government, so social development was stunted and the seeds of disaffection sown. This then meant that the military had to remain to suppress rebellion and organize government.

Economic exchange was clearly very important as the Roman army brought with it very substantial spending power. Locally a fort had two kinds of impact. Its large population needed food and other supplies. Some of these were certainly brought from long distances, but demands were inevitably placed on the local area. Although goods could be requisitioned, they were usually paid for and this probably stimulated changes in the local economy. When not campaigning, soldiers needed to be occupied, otherwise they represented a potentially dangerous source of friction and disloyalty. Hence at Vindolanda one of the writing-tablets dated 25 April tells of 343 men engaged on tasks like shoemaking, building a bathhouse, operating kilns, digging clay and working lead. Such activities had a major effect on the local area, in particular with the construction of infrastructure such as roads, which improved access to hitherto remote areas.

Each soldier in a fort received his pay, but in regions without a developed economy there was initially little on which it could be spent. The pool of excess cash rapidly stimulated the growth of a thriving economy outside fort gates. Some of the demand for the services and goods was no doubt fulfilled by people drawn from far afield, but some local people certainly became entwined in this new

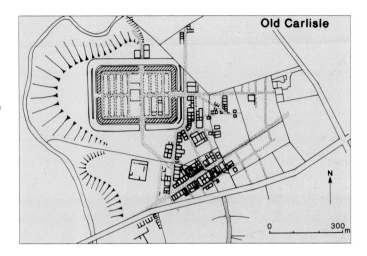

62 *(right)* Plan showing the auxiliary fort at Old Carlisle in Cumbria together with the *vicus*, or settlement, around it. The fort *vicus* provided services for the military but probably also attracted business from the surrounding area so that it effectively became a town.

63 *(below)* Tombstone from Aquileia in northern Italy commemorating an officer of a British auxiliary unit. Local recruitment means that it is difficult to establish whether an individual soldier was a Briton or from elsewhere. This man's name may suggest that he was from the Danube region, illustrating the social mixing that characterized the Roman Empire. In translation the tombstone reads: 'To Lucius Julius Pansa retired centurion of the first cohort of Britons. Gaius Julius Proculus, his heir, set this up according to the provisions of the will.'

economy. There was informal marriage with soldiers, who until Septimius Severus' reform of 197 were not legally entitled to wed, and whole new communities grew up in the fort *vici* (**62**). These settlements acted like the small towns of the civil zone, becoming centres for artisan and trading populations.

The army also provided a means of personal advancement outside the native hierarchy. On retirement after service in an auxiliary regiment a man obtained hereditary Roman citizenship. Auxiliary soldiers were recruited from the native peoples and many of the earliest units established bore names taken from either the native leaders who raised them or the tribes from which they were first raised.

Once in existence a unit recruited on an *ad hoc* basis from the area in which it was stationed and there was evidently large-scale individual recruitment within Britain. The total numbers involved were at least 12,500 men up to the reign of Hadrian, with a peak around AD 80. Although a very small proportion of the total population, this perhaps had a massive local impact when a large proportion of the young men were removed from an area. Newly raised regiments were normally transferred to another province from whence it was unlikely that individual recruits would ever return (**63**). Most units raised in Britain went to the Danube or Rhine although one is recorded in Morocco. The reverse process brought young men to Britain where many continued to live after their 20 to 25 years' service, and this added to the cosmopolitan Roman character of the frontier population. By the later Roman period, frontier garrisons were only rarely transferred from area to area, service in units became effectively hereditary and the forts were no longer manned at full strength.

64 *(right)* Reconstruction drawing showing the hall built on top of a Roman granary, which was within the fort at Birdoswold on Hadrian's Wall. Excavations at this site have shown that occupation here carried on long after AD 410. Continued occupation of forts within the frontier region suggests that they remained centres of power into the sub-Roman period.

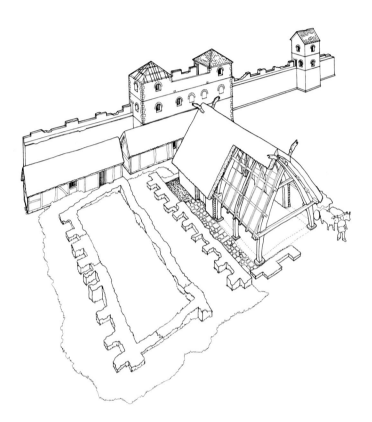

This process of settling in as a community over successive generations, combined with local recruitment, presumably accounts for the apparent stability of the British northern frontier in the later Roman period. It also explains why some of the forts continued in occupation long after Rome's writ ceased to have any formal meaning in Britain, at the beginning of the fifth century (**64**). The circumstances that had allowed natives to become Romanized also led the self-sustaining military community of the frontier area to become effectively British.

IMPERIAL DEMANDS

The creation of the Roman empire resulted from political rivalry within an intensely competitive society at Rome, where status and wealth were acquired and maintained by military aggrandizement. The spiral of internal competition brought external aggression and the resultant wars led to the acquisition of new territories. Victory also brought wealth to the conquerors, both from the booty of conquest and through the subsequent exploitation of the territories by crude extortion, commerce and taxation. This incoming wealth caused the centre of the empire to become highly dependent on the continuation of Roman expansion and the consequent accumulation of wealth. It created an Italian economy in which land became increasingly valuable, but where the production of agricultural staples was decreasingly important. Italy thus became dependent on her overseas territories for commodities like grain, vital if the urban population was to be fed and thus kept peaceful. To guarantee the flow of staple foods Rome increased the regulation of supply, with the result that a complex centralized economy developed in the Mediterranean. How far these imperial demands reached out to her farthest provinces is not clear. We can be certain that immediately after the conquest Britain was subjected first to asset-stripping, as valuables were removed by the army, and then to economic exploitation, as traders followed in the wake of the Roman invasion.

We cannot estimate the amount of bullion taken as booty but, given the large quantities of gold and silver coinage and the presence of gold artefacts such as torcs which circulated in Late Iron Age Britain, it would be a mistake to underestimate the bullion removed by the Romans. The 1990 find of torcs from Snettisham in Norfolk is a reminder of the volume of wealth circulating in Iron Age Britain (see **83**). That site alone has produced enough gold to have paid a unit of Roman auxiliary troops for just over a year.

The attractions of Britain for traders in the wake of the invasion are more easily assessed. There were not only possibilities of obtaining raw materials and selling goods to the natives on highly advantageous terms, but there were also the salaries of the soldiers themselves. The empire redistributed wealth between different areas through taxation and payments of state dues. Taxes were raised from across the empire although the burden was not even. Italy was undertaxed, and exemptions were occasionally granted to peoples who had helped Rome during her expansion. Outside Italy there was probably a fairly even burden, although in newly acquired territories it took time for regular taxation to be established following a census and the establishment of collection systems.

The largest single item of Roman expenditure was army pay. Not only can we estimate each soldier's annual pay but we also understand the uneven disposition of the army across the empire.

Soldiers were mainly stationed around the edges of the empire, in provinces like Britain, which contained about 10 per cent of the whole Roman army in the first century AD. One economic result of this was a net redistribution of wealth from central tax-paying provinces to those in which the army was located. Thus the army that conquered Britain cost Rome the equivalent of about 2,000 kg (2 tons) of gold per year in pay alone.

The arrival of this cash almost certainly destabilized Britain's economy. It had previously been largely under the control of local aristocrats and was relatively small scale. At first this vast inflow of cash cannot have been met by an equivalent expansion in the production of goods for sale. In such a classic inflationary situation those with goods to sell were able to obtain increasingly higher prices for them. A price differential thus developed between goods in the new province and those in adjacent regions. The massive profits from trading in these circumstances accounts for the influx of goods, such as pottery from Gaul. Such low-value commodities were not generally traded over long distances, as the profit margin was insufficient to justify their transport. In the newly conquered province not only could a high price be asked but also scarcity in the preceding period had given Roman goods a cachet as status symbols. Thus trade thrived to the financial benefit of overseas traders (**65**). This probably explains London's very rapid development around AD 50 when the port emerged as the main centre where overseas traders established themselves.

How far post-conquest trade infiltrated native society is unclear. Although Roman goods spread very rapidly so that samian ware, for instance, appeared on the vast majority of native sites in the south and east by 70, we do not know how this happened. It is unlikely that the influx of Roman money and goods led to a wholesale and immediate breakdown in the native economy. It is more likely that a separate Roman economy grew rapidly under the control of overseas traders, who lived in places like London and around the installations of army and government, while also dealing with native peoples. Meanwhile the Iron Age elites maintained their control over traditional economic networks as their territories were transformed into *civitates*. This control enabled them to deal directly with incoming traders who did business without totally disrupting society. This is seen in areas like Sussex where Roman

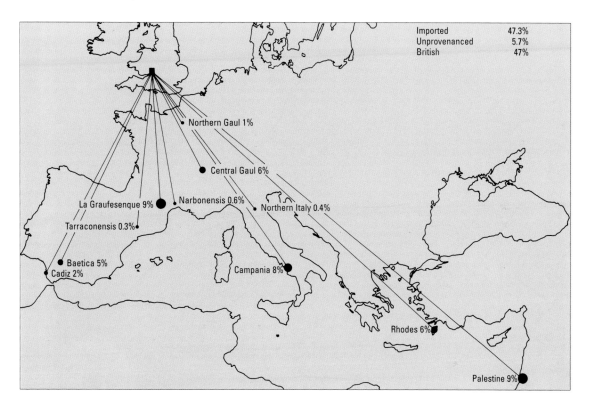

Imported   47.3%
Unprovenanced   5.7%
British   47%

Northern Gaul 1%

Central Gaul 6%

La Graufesenque 9%   Narbonensis 0.6%

Tarraconensis 0.3%   Northern Italy 0.4%

Baetica 5%
Cadiz 2%   Campania 8%

Rhodes 6%

Palestine 9%

65 *(above)* Map showing the various sources that supplied pottery to the Roman fort at Kingsholm, Gloucester, during the period AD 50-60. By examining the clay fabric from which pots were made it is often possible to establish where they were manufactured. The widespread movement of large volumes of goods such as wine and olive oil was characteristic of the Roman Empire and this trade is easily mapped using such pottery. As the province developed, Roman Britain became more self-sufficient in goods like ordinary household pottery (see 39) so the levels of importation fell.

goods came first to the principal native sites and only later percolated down to the ordinary people. Although this change appears rapid to us, to contemporaries the generation or so that it took to happen was long enough for leading natives to adjust their control to the new circumstances.

The character of Roman money supports the idea that the economy was under social control and not simply a free market. After the conquest, coinage spread through the countryside only slowly and in large denominations inappropriate for most day-to-day transactions. This coinage could have been used for buying and selling but only when large consolidated debts needed to be paid off. The supply of coinage was also very uneven. Shortages of coin and vast fluctuations in volume of supply imply that arbitrary administrative decisions rather than economic necessities governed the supply of money, and also suggest that coinage was not widely used in the market place. We should probably not see the economy of Roman Britain as a modern free market, but as a hybrid in which most day-to-day business relied on traditional modes of barter, exchange and indebtedness. Such practices worked well in small-scale societies when they were maintained by the authority of the tribe and where each person knew those with whom they were dealing. Only where transactions involved the Roman State or strangers did other systems need to operate. It was in these circumstances that the use of coinage probably became essential.

The most important transactions to involve coinage were tax payments. In the early empire taxes were assessed and paid in bullion (in gold or silver coin). In a few areas payments were instead collected in goods like ox hides, or could be substituted by the provision of military recruits, presumably because the economy was underdeveloped. Taxes in kind were probably convenient to the government in areas where the army was based. However, they were cumbersome to administer and highly inconvenient where the goods needed moving over longer distances. They may well have existed in some parts of Britain, but where we have no evidence to the contrary we should probably assume that payment was in cash. The principal taxes were a land tax and a poll tax, assessed for each local government area through a periodic census. Each *civitas* was responsible for the collection and delivery of taxes to the procurator. Additional levies, such as customs dues on trade between provinces and inheritance tax, were collected centrally. Municipal magistrates were personally liable for tax collection and the payment of any shortfall, which ensured that they were assiduous. Individuals had to obtain cash to pay their taxes and this provided the main motive for becoming involved in the coin-using economy. Goods were sold to obtain low-value bronze coins, which were accumulated and exchanged for the bullion coins needed to settle with the taxman. A major effect of this tax regime was to concentrate social and economic control in the hands of the municipal authorities.

After the initial inrush of money, traders and goods following the invasion there was a period of economic adjustment. Soon after Rome's arrival, metal resources known before the conquest were exploited, initially by the State (see **40**). Lead ores, containing silver, were extracted in the Mendips by 49, and similar exploitation later took place in Derbyshire, Yorkshire, north Wales and the Welsh Marches. Lead was the less valuable by-product of silver production, and it was this bullion in which Rome was most interested. We cannot reliably estimate the bullion yield and subsequent workings have obscured most Roman operations. As

66 *(below)* A cast of the decoration on a pot from Corbridge, Northumberland. It shows the figure of a blacksmith working at an anvil. This representation provides a rare view of one of the important craft industries that became widespread in the province under Roman rule. Smiths were believed to have supernatural powers and this particular image probably had divine overtones.

many of the silver mines stayed under direct government control until the second century the bullion recovered was presumably of value. Later some mines were let to private contractors suggesting that their production of bullion might have decreased, although it may simply have proved more profitable to accept a guaranteed income from a contractor rather than rely on a variable return from direct exploitation.

The only gold-mining we can be sure of was at Dolaucothi in southwest Wales and was certainly under military control since a fort was built at nearby Pumpsaint to oversee it. Operations began around 75 and involved both underground mines and open-workings on the hillside. The volume of production is impossible to judge although the scale of infrastructure shows that it cannot have been insignificant.

The other principal mineral often mentioned is Cornish tin. Many believe that this had been exploited in the Iron Age and traded with Phoenicians and then Romans travelling from Spain. The literary evidence for this tin trade is partly mythological; there is not yet any archaeological evidence of Iron Age mining and Rome seems not to have exploited the tin until the later period. The only evidence for official tinworking comes from a phase of road construction during the third century and a fourth-century ingot bearing an official stamp.

Copper was certainly being mined in Wales early in the Roman period, although its exploitation was undertaken by private companies who leased the rights from the State. Minerals were in heavy demand since there was an enormous increase in everyday metal use in the Roman period when contrasted with the Iron Age. Civilian demand was clearly considerably larger than the State's needs, so native mining and metal production presumably grew to satisfy the new demand.

The same is true for iron, which was manufactured and worked at many places (**66**). Most production was in private hands and working was on a modest scale. The military needed plenty of iron and this accounts for their strong connection with the large-scale iron industry that developed in the Weald of Sussex and Kent from the later first century. Here several production sites were associated with the naval fleet (the *classis Britannica*), which was based at Boulogne but used ports in the southeast including Dover.

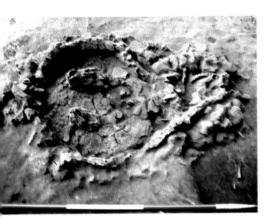

67 *(above)* The excavated foundations of a kiln for the production of pottery, found at Holme-upon-Spalding Moor in East Yorkshire. The kiln comprised a simple dome-shaped clay oven with a single flue (right). The pottery produced was the everyday type used for cooking. The growth of industries producing such products was typical of Roman Britain and illustrates the development of a widespread consumer economy. At this rural site pottery manufacture probably took place in addition to farming, using local raw materials and the labour available at the slack times of year.

Elsewhere both smithing and small-scale smelting have been found on many settlement sites showing that both the material and the technology had become universally available. Some demand was met from local ore sources, which are now exhausted but were then sufficient to meet local requirements.

Local production of Roman-style goods spread over a wide area of Britain and the full range of sites in the most Romanized areas was well supplied with them. This is best illustrated by the most common everyday items such as pottery, produced in the new styles in Britain very soon after the conquest. Large numbers of tablewares continued to be imported until the end of the second century, but local production rapidly became normal for everyday use (**67**). Production centres first grew up close to the new public towns. The distributions of pots manufactured near towns and used in surrounding areas map the places from which people came to a town. This was generally within a radius of about 15 km (9 miles). This represents the size of area a town normally served so it is significant that when small towns also emerged as distribution centres they too reached similar distributions.

The spread of everyday objects was often influenced by the social affinities of buyers and sellers. A number of distribution patterns of objects, varying from pots and personal ornaments to mosaic pavement designs, were confined to individual *civitas* territories. This was sometimes simply because people obtained goods at the town they most frequently visited or where they had a tribal affinity, but the use of particular designs of objects was perhaps also an expression of belonging to a particular social group. In a number of cultures everyday objects are used as cultural markers in this way. This apparently also happened in Roman Britain where the change from a tribal society to one integrated into the empire was neither instantaneous nor complete.

After the first century there was an accelerating trend away from a reliance on imported goods and towards larger-scale domestic production. The decline in overseas trade was partly a result of the levelling out of economic imbalances across the empire. With the growth of Britain's economy, the quick profits made in the immediate aftermath of Roman conquest could no longer be exploited. Moreover, local products undercut the prices of imports, which were made more expensive by the cost of their transport. As the province's economy grew so tax income rose, and as the size of the imperial army stationed here declined, the imbalance between tax revenue and expenditure evened out. As a consequence of this, the opportunities for highly profitable trading by outsiders were significantly reduced.

At the same time industries established in the wake of the invasion thrived, taking an increasingly large share of the province's market. The most successful pottery industries were those that produced higher-quality products similar to those previously imported. Their production centres are distinguished by rural locations near *civitas* boundaries. Positioned away from *civitas* centres their products were acceptable to more than a single ethnic group. These locations certainly increased the potential market available and enabled them to achieve greater success than competitors who traded within a single *civitas*. Several successful producers were also positioned on navigable rivers to reduce their distribution costs. Although the road network was good, it was slow and expensive for bulk transport and archaeological research suggests that river transport was at least half the price of road haulage. River barges also had a larger capacity, making distribution more effective, especially for a fragile commodity like pottery where breakage rates on roads were most likely great.

Even with the development of major regional industries in fourth-century Britain there was probably not a sufficiently continuous and ready supply of goods to allow a free market to develop fully. The range of objects on an individual settlement was as much a result of availability as of rational marketing choice. Although by the mid-fourth century the economy was more self-sufficient than it had been in the first, it seems not to have achieved full maturity. Economic development had clear advantages for the inhabitants of the province and the most privileged people were living well. However, unlike the first century, little obvious financial benefit accrued to the rest of the empire.

There was also an alteration in tax collection. The inflation of the third century reduced the real value of cash taxes at the time when governments were too weak to raise their levels. The shortfall in resources resulting from this imbalance was not fully resolved until well into the fourth century. In the interim the needs of the State were met by collecting taxes in kind. These exactions were drawn from the provincials who were required to deliver products such as corn to collection points so that they could be used by the army. The shift towards this mode of taxation probably slowed the economy by removing goods from circulation while the direct collection of taxes reduced the reliance of the system on the *civitates,* and lessened the central roles of the public towns as economic and social centres. The *civitas* magistrates lost social influence, as they no longer held the same central control over tax collection, which came to be supervised by civil servants.

The other important feature of the taxation system was created by uneven collection. Although the level of Roman taxation was modest, at perhaps only 10 per cent of production, the burden was uneven. In the early empire when organized through the municipalities, the rich who held power were also responsible for tax collection. They are unlikely to have shouldered the burden themselves. At the best they paid an equal share, and are more likely to have manipulated the system to pay less than others. In the later empire opportunities to avoid the payment of taxes by serving as a civil servant were open only to the richer *honestiores,* so the aggregate tax burden fell more heavily on the remainder of society. Moreover there was a wide variety of tax exemptions. These were of the greatest value to the wealthiest who received the largest tax demands. These people were also most successful in refusing or deferring payment so that the real burden actually fell increasingly on the poor and weak.

These trends, however minor, combine to show that the Roman taxation system was regressive, permitting more and more wealth to accumulate in the hands of fewer and fewer people. The growth of a larger peasant underclass and a thriving aristocracy in fourth-century Britain resulted in part from taxation gradually shifting the balance of wealth to favour the rich, especially after any outward flow of cash to the centre of the empire had ceased. After the third century the structure of the Roman empire was increasingly regional and beneficial to the local aristocracies.

ART: CELTIC TRADITIONS AND THEIR ROMANIZATION

68 *(above)* Celtic design on the back of a Late Iron Age mirror from Birdlip, Gloucestershire. The design is characteristic of Celtic art, showing a liveliness that is actually produced by a very careful layout with complex symmetry.

There is a wealth of artistic and architectural material from Roman Britain. It varies in scale and magnificence from small decorated bronzes to Roman architectural monuments. These were not created in isolation but were a product of social tensions and the individual aspirations of the inhabitants. As such they bring us much closer to an understanding of society than other sources. However, the objects cannot tell their own stories but have to be explained in relation to ideas about their creators and users. This is rarely unambiguous and individual items often had a variety of meanings. A decorated Celtic shield may have been an emblem of power to a native warrior but became a symbol of victory when captured and placed in a Roman temple. We thus need to examine the objects and the ideas that help us to understand them.

The term 'Celtic' is widely used to describe the peoples of central and northwestern Europe during later prehistory, but is rather ill defined and conveys a variety of different meanings. Some use it to describe peoples of today who speak languages such as Welsh and Breton. Others employ it to denote a people who migrated into Europe during prehistory. Finally it also signifies an artistic style used during the Iron Age. Any of these uses is legitimate as long as we are aware that an artistic style implies neither a common ethnic origin nor a language. As patterns of human societies differ widely it is extremely unwise to take evidence about Celtic society from one place, such as Gaul at the time of Caesar, and use it to explain patterns in other areas that lack documentation.

I use the term Celtic to describe the artistic style widespread on the eve of the Roman conquest and which remained of significance throughout the Roman occupation. It used predominantly abstract designs that combined complex symmetry with sophisticated techniques of infilling spaces within designs (**68**). Most of the surviving examples are on metalwork: designs covered the backs of mirrors and adorned armour, shields and helmets as well as the surfaces of smaller everyday items like brooches.

This style had a long pedigree having spread across central and western Europe from about 1000 BC. The artistic ideas perhaps first came with peoples from the east, but the style later spread as it was copied by indigenous peoples. Different regions periodically experienced a particular artistic vigour when styles evolved to reach new peaks of achievement. By the time of the conquest it was neither dominant nor vigorous on the European mainland although in Britain it was flourishing with an especial dynamism.

It is rarely easy to date pieces of Celtic art so there are differences of interpretation. Some see the flowering of Celtic art in Britain as a last flourish of native culture in free areas of Europe before it was extinguished by the dead hand of the Roman State. I prefer to see it as the product of a society rapidly evolving under the stimulus of Rome's proximity. This created the artistic environment in which Celtic art reached its apogee, and many of the finest objects reached a Roman clientele after the invasion. What survives is probably not a representative selection of all that was produced. Where organic materials have survived they carry the same decoration so we can guess that other media such as textiles were often also highly patterned (**69**). The most spectacular objects were not typical, being produced for the leaders of society. Surviving metalwork is dominated by objects associated with horse-riding and by items like harnesses and decorative fittings for chariots. Other media were personal ornaments and warrior equipment, drinking equipment and mirrors, but these are far less common.

The objects varied, but the types of decoration were remarkably similar. There was a strong preference for symmetrically balanced curved designs that combined scrolls with circles. Infills were sophisticated and either engraved or filled with inlaid glasses or enamels. Circular designs and complex symmetrical patterns were laid out using compasses and their designs clearly convey the technical and artistic skills applied. Surfaces were generally two-dimensional but the techniques employed make them stand out and provide a vigorous three-dimensional character. Highly abstract human and animal forms occur but the principal emphasis was on abstract images whose restrained style transmits a lively tension. Individual features were sometimes derived from the art of the Classical world but they had undergone major mutations. The essence was the combination of careful abstract design with intricately executed detail producing an overall impression of balanced and lively simplicity. Its producers were both artistically inspired and technically brilliant.

Their skills should not lead us to treat the art in an unduly modern way. The styles and items selected for elaborate treatment were the product of a relationship between artist and patron. The existence of professional artists signifies a society sufficiently

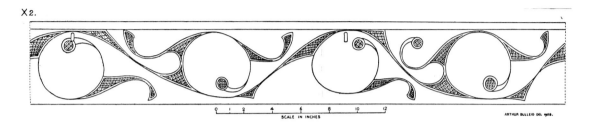

69 *(above)* Celtic ornament on a wooden vessel from the Iron Age lake village at Glastonbury, Somerset. This rare survival demonstrates how ornamentation similar to that on the metalwork was probably widely used on organic materials in everyday use.

sophisticated and stable to nurture and support them. Their patrons were aristocrats who used art to display their social prestige. Although artists were directly responsible for the style used, their choice was prescribed by social expectations, which also influenced a patron's requirements. Items of personal adornment or for decorating horses or carts show how power and prestige were associated with warrior display and the use of horses or chariots. The arms and armour produced were not always fully functional but this does not lessen their impact. The message was that the status of those in power was ultimately underwritten by military might. Equally their magnificence showed that they had the wealth to support the finest craftsmen. The use of decorated drinking vessels, wine containers and mirrors also set apart the leaders and enabled them to display their status to social inferiors and outsiders.

While patronage and social convention defined the kinds of object decorated, individual artists were presumably responsible for the conceptualization and detail of the designs used. Even with this freedom there was sufficient homogeneity to identify a uniformity of Celtic style. The strong similarities between individual decorative items suggest that the art contained symbolism and perhaps coded meanings. We might expect, for instance, that certain designs were used to identify particular tribal groups, social strata, or the membership of certain gender, marital or age sets (**69**).

We must also take account of artists' perceptions. We are inclined to judge Celtic portrayals of the human figure by comparison with our expectations of how the human form should be represented, judging deviations as either primitivism or abstract stylization (**70**). Celtic artists probably saw the world in a different way; we should thus use the art to see the world through their eyes.

The most spectacular pieces which best illustrate the period have only very rarely been recovered from ordinary excavated settlements,

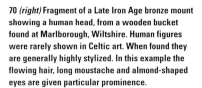

70 *(right)* Fragment of a Late Iron Age bronze mount showing a human head, from a wooden bucket found at Marlborough, Wiltshire. Human figures were rarely shown in Celtic art. When found they are generally highly stylized. In this example the flowing hair, long moustache and almond-shaped eyes are given particular prominence.

presumably because most were highly prized and infrequently lost. Settlement finds are generally either small pieces, like decorated horse harnesses, or fragments, perhaps scrap intended for reworking. Complete objects have been found away from settlements, often by chance rather than through systematic archaeological exploration. Some came from hoards, others from deposits at temples or in graves, and many during the dredging of rivers.

Many of these finds result from the careful deposition of objects that had a high social value. Those from rivers are too frequent to be anything other than deliberate deposits. This pattern can only be fully appreciated in the context of religious practice (see Chapter 5). The placing of valued objects in wet places and in hoards occurred from the Bronze Age onwards. Such acts combined veneration of the gods with rituals that established the donor's social position.

THE IMPACT OF THE CONQUEST

Before and during the conquest society was presumably under stress induced by the Roman threat. This was felt both through Rome's interference from Caesar onwards, and by the rapid social evolution stimulated by Rome's proximity. Internal conflict was generated as tribes expanded their territories at the expense of neighbours. Under these conditions it perhaps became increasingly important to display group identity. Similar periods of stress elsewhere have led closer definition and bolder statements of identity to develop. The florescence of Celtic art in Late Iron Age Britain may thus have resulted from social stresses brought about by the increasing proximity of Rome. As Rome loomed closer and Gauls themselves

71 *(above)* Stone slab from the Roman fort at Binchester, Co. Durham. This is a typical example of Romano-British sculpture, which appears dull and mechanical in contrast to the Celtic art of the Iron Age. In translation the text reads: 'To Aesculapius and Salus for the welfare of the cavalry regiment of Vettonians, Roman citizens. Marcus Aurelius [...] ocomas, doctor, willingly and deservedly fulfilled his vow.'

became more Romanized, the inhabitants of Britain perhaps felt an increasing need to demonstrate their Celtic identities. Similarly, powerful leaders found it more desirable to emphasize their social positions both to warring neighbours and to their social inferiors. Celtic art was thus both an expression of native identity and a response to the nearing Roman presence.

Given the dynamism of native art on the eve of the conquest its subsequent decline appears perplexing (**71**). Why should a community of artists who produced such brilliant work suddenly seem incapable of producing, as R.G. Collingwood put it, 'anything that rises above the level of dull, mechanical imitation to that of even third-rate artistic achievement'? There was some continuation of traditions, not only beyond the Roman province where the style continued to flourish, but also within the conquered territories. The range of objects changed with more emphasis placed on personal dress ornaments. We also see the use of Celtic techniques in the decoration of Roman military equipment. The conquerors evidently valued the aesthetic qualities of native craft and wished to amalgamate it with their own traditions. Roman art had a strong tradition of gathering together the best of native traditions. Soldiers were not provided with military equipment from central workshops but were instead responsible for the acquisition of their own personal gear and the majority were recruited from the northwestern provinces. Their choice of Celtic styles for the decoration of military equipment may thus have its origins in the tastes of the Celtic rather than the Roman world (**72**).

Despite this continuity the native community was exposed to a range of new styles and media including stone and metal sculpture, monumental architecture, floor mosaic and wall painting. Many items of Roman art are often seen as second-rate copies of Greek originals. The art of Roman Britain is thus often adversely compared with that of both Classical Mediterranean prototypes and its Celtic predecessors. This impedes a fuller understanding of the changes that characterized the period and overlooks the ways in which Classical ideas and religious practices became widely established among the peoples of Britain.

Roman annexation had a traumatic effect on the native aristocracy. For those who survived in power, status and prestige remained important but could no longer be expressed in the same

72 *(above)* Two copper alloy, horse-harness mounts illustrating the use of enamel in Celtic metalwork. The example on the left (from London) has a carefully developed design with much of the surface infilled with coloured glass. The example on the right (from the Polden Hills hoard in Somerset) has a more restrained design in which the enamel is used to contrast with the plain metal surfaces. Both examples probably date to the middle of the first century AD. As these styles of decoration came to appear on some Roman military equipment, we cannot be certain the ethnic origins of those who used these objects.

ways. Power was no longer military although many remained as civil leaders in the new *civitates*. The military initiative had passed to the imperial army and instead native leaders held only administrative power, exercised at the absolute discretion of Rome and discharged through the new urban centres alien to native traditions. The former symbols of power were thus undercut. Highly decorated arms, armour and horse gear were no longer appropriate. Rome's new emblems were rapidly adopted across the conquered lands. Those in power under the new regime wished to impress both the conquerors and their social inferiors with their new Roman values. Adoption of Latin, and Roman styles of dress and living (including its architecture and interior decoration), show that they aspired to their conquerors' values and demonstrated to ordinary people that their leaders were now identified with the new regime. The new Roman styles thus served to re-establish the social positions of the tribal leaders and replaced Celtic symbols.

The influences that determined what native leaders adopted as models of Roman culture are thus very important. A visitor from Rome might have seen Britain as extremely provincial, but what passed here as 'Roman' was sufficient to identify a Briton with the new regime. Objects and ideas arrived first with the Roman army, then small quantities of goods came with administrators, and a larger number were brought by traders. Some of these people came from the Mediterranean, but the majority originated in the nearer provinces. Four of five legions during the first century came from the Rhineland, the fifth from the Danube. Similar origins account for

73 *(above)* Life-size marble sculpture of the head of a child from the villa at Fishbourne, West Sussex, dated to the late first century AD. Naturalistic representation of the human form was characteristic of the art of the Mediterranean world but new to Britain.

74 *(below)* Central medallion on the pediment of the temple of Sulis Minerva at Bath (75). The high quality of the stone-carving, probably undertaken by artists from northern Gaul in AD 60–80, is evident. The central figure shows a vigorous portrait of a bearded Medusa.

most auxiliary troops stationed here. Many of the influences were not directly Roman, but came from second-generation Romanized provincials. Existing cultural links between southern Britain, Gaul and Germany may have contributed to the rapid changes here.

Cultural influences were of three types: the bringing of objects, the transfer of craftworkers and the import of ideas. Many objects were not art in even the broadest sense and comprised utilitarian items of clothing, utensils and equipment. We should not underestimate the social cachet associated with such mundane possessions that had not previously been available. The flooding of Britain with red-gloss pottery from Gaul, decorated with scenes of Classical mythology, probably brought many into contact with the styles and artistic concepts of the Greco-Roman world for the first time, whether or not the symbolism was understood. Mass-produced goods were accompanied by fewer more aesthetically impressive objects such as statuettes (**91**). Some such pieces perhaps first came with officials for their own religious worship; others were then acquired by indigenous leaders as diplomatic gifts, as presents or by purchase. Once seen by the natives, such objects created a fashion that rapidly spread through the province.

In the most extreme instances they literally bought the whole package of Roman culture. The Fishbourne villa, built in the third quarter of the first century AD, probably for the native client king Cogidubnus, amply illustrates his Roman pretensions. It was constructed in the latest Italian style with imported marbles and stylish mosaics. It was lavishly furnished with imported sculptures and other Classical objects (**73**). A visitor from Rome would have recognized its owner as a participant in the contemporary culture of the empire, not at all provincial in taste. Even if those from the traditional families looked down on him as *nouveau riche,* they will have been unable to dismiss him as uncultured. Although exceptional, this demonstrates how new cultural symbols bound provincials to the identity of the Roman world.

Such examples established a standard to be copied. One result was an influx of craftworkers, particularly those skilled in artistic media like stone-carving, which had not existed before the conquest. Civilian workers came mostly from Gaul and Germany. The magnificent temple built beside the sacred spring at Bath was constructed only about twenty years after the conquest (**74, 75**). Its

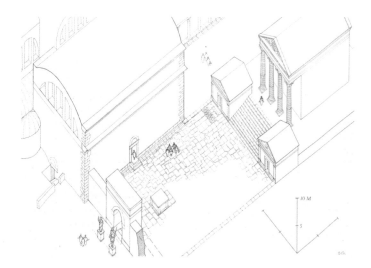

75 *(right)* The forecourt temple of Sulis Minerva at Bath as it may have appeared in the second century AD. The temple to the right faces the sacred square with the altar axially between it and the main entrance. Another axis through the altar, at right angles to the first, points to the opening to the sacred hot-water spring, which was enclosed beneath a vaulted roof. This spring was evidently a place for the deposition of gifts to the goddess (see 90). The architectural decoration of the temple is most closely paralleled in northern Gaul and it is believed that artists from there were brought to Britain for its construction around AD 60–80 (see 74).

detail shows that it was carved by artists from northeast Gaul. In the absence of a tradition of Classical stone-carving and building the desire to develop Roman amenities will have been difficult to fulfil. Administrators thus used their personal contacts to put the Britons in touch with architects and masons. As many of the officials in Britain had strong links with Gaul, it is not surprising that early Roman Britain owes much to craftworkers from that area. Local workshops did develop and stylistically similar groups of sculpture show how skills in this new medium became widespread. Similarly skills in the use of mosaic, wall painting, ceramic decoration and metal-working developed throughout the province with the eventual emergence of characteristically Romano-British styles (**76**).

This art had a major impact on the native peoples but the transformation that occurred is easy to overlook. One of the most important factors was a change in scale. The Iron Age world was highly localized, with people rarely travelling far beyond their own region and those who did seldom going beyond the shores of Britain. On occasions large groups amassed for war or religious festivals, but society remained centred on small communities. Iron Age architecture reflected this with even the largest of the *oppida* and hill-forts containing no more than clusters of medium-sized structures. The spaces inside even the largest roundhouses were modest, and the use of rounded shapes and organic building materials gave buildings a human scale.

Incorporation in the Roman world brought a change difficult to envisage. The Roman army was divided into units, the smallest of which generally comprised 500 men. Legions were ten times that size, so their camps were the equivalent of the largest settlements

76 *(right)* A tile found at Neatham, Hampshire, with a portrait of a woman that was scratched on to it while wet. The doodle appears to have begun as a drawing of a pot and was then altered to show a woman's face. The staring eyes are characteristic of Celtic art. The picture gives a rare glimpse of how the indigenous population saw the world.

previously seen in Britain. They were first built with leather tents, but temporary encampments were soon replaced by permanent bases with rectangular timber buildings arrayed in a rectangular street grid with major buildings at the centre. For the average Briton the impact of these forts can scarcely have been less awe-inspiring than the sight of a fully equipped army unit marching across the countryside or the construction of unerringly straight roads, with which the invaders changed the geography and joined hitherto unconnected areas.

This impact was perhaps insignificant compared with the effects of civil architecture as towns came to dominate the province. The largest public buildings were alien in both style and scale. Most native buildings had been relatively small with poorly lit interiors, so the sheer size of space enclosed within buildings like the basilica of London must have been astonishing (see **49**). Never before had people experienced a roofed space containing such a huge volume with a soaring interior lit from high up. We cannot begin to imagine the impact of such architecture on those never previously exposed to it. This was an architecture of dominance in which subject peoples were literally made to feel small by buildings that epitomized imperial power. Supremacy was accentuated by the unyielding straight lines of both individual buildings and planned settlements since these too provided a marked contrast with the natural curvilinear shapes dominant in the native realm.

This domination perhaps led to the rapid adoption of Roman architecture by a native aristocracy concerned to maintain and enhance their superiority. The new-built environment of both towns and country, constructed within a couple of generations of the invasion, illustrates their employment of Roman symbolism for personal ends.

THE QUALITY OF ROMANO-BRITISH ART

The artistic styles of Roman Britain have not attracted aesthetic acclaim. Romano-British sculpture, for instance, appears provincial and failed to fulfil Greco-Roman ideals of naturalism (see **71**). Such judgements do not view the material on its own terms. Native sculptors learned their skills from outsiders and anyone who has tried to carve stone will know that it requires immense skill. Mistakes could be made, resulting in the miscarving of a letter or the splitting of a stone, but the end-product was unlikely to be very different from what was intended. Sculpture is not like other media such as painting where a serious mistake can be overpainted, so a finished piece needs to be judged on the assumption that it was more or less satisfactory to both patron and artist. Working from this assumption we may consider why the results often fail to fulfil our expectations of successful art.

A patron probably had little knowledge of the art at the centre of the Roman world. The choice of a particular form, for instance a Classical god, shows an aspiration towards Roman taste. Unfamiliarity with Classical models and ideals perhaps contributed towards a failure to distinguish between good and bad art. What was important was that the subject-matter and form were 'Roman' in taste. The aesthetic qualities or success of the work were not so easy to judge and perhaps had only a secondary importance. The artist's commission was to produce a Classical object and details of style are unlikely to have been specified. In copying ideas or objects to fulfil the commission artists were prisoners of their own perceptions. The key was the artist's way of seeing the world, which was probably different from that of someone brought up in the Classical tradition. We should thus look at Romano-British sculpture as a product of a Celtic perception of the Classical ideas. British carvings of Roman gods often lacked Classical proportions but were sufficiently similar to the models to have satisfied a patron's naturalistic tastes. This is surely understandable in a society without either photographic images or previous familiarity with naturalistic art.

77 *(right)* A sculptured gravestone from Murrell Hill, Carlisle, probably dating to the second century AD, which provides an example of Romano-British stone-carving at its best. The Classical, naturalistic form of the figure is combined with an interest in the shapes and lines to create an almost abstract design.

Unfamiliarity with Classical ideals was perhaps even more important to the artist, who presumably wished to produce aesthetically fulfilling work as well as to satisfy the commission. Rather than looking at a Romano-British sculpture of a god as a naturalistic representation of the human form, we should view it as a combination of shapes, an abstract pattern using different forms of infill to catch the light and create interesting shapes (77). When we do this (remembering that sculptures were originally often brightly painted), we can begin to appreciate a style derived from Celtic metalwork but now transformed into a medium satisfactory to the requirements of Romanized patrons. While perhaps not as satisfying as the earlier metalwork, these sculptures may then be read in the same way.

Stone sculpture was not the most successful medium for these ideas, but other arts achieved a more satisfactory aesthetic balance, combining Celtic ways of seeing with Roman forms. Most notable were mosaic pavements, which reached their zenith during the fourth century (**57, 78**). These pavements often illustrate the successful use of a narrow range of colour within abstract and repetitive designs. This produced far more satisfying works, although very different from the finely made and detailed pavements containing human and animal figures seen in other provinces. Where attempts were made at the representation of figures they too were for Celtic rather than Classical eyes (**76, 79**). Through them we glimpse a different ideal of beauty to that represented by a Classical Venus or Hercules.

In the other decorative arts, especially metal-working, Britain produced objects which stand comparison with those from anywhere. The arts of the silversmith were cosmopolitan and those with the wealth to patronize them had developed tastes. A number of significant silver vessels probably manufactured in Britain betray the tastes of their patrons and show that exceptionally skilled smiths were at work here (**80**). The most magnificent objects show mythological scenes that demonstrate the Classical learning of the wealthiest inhabitants. Few items of silver plate from Britain do not derive from hoards, and there are interesting parallels with Iron Age metalwork. Why the hoards were buried is something of a mystery: while a few were obviously to be used as bullion – where the plate was chopped into pieces – the burial of others, such as that found at Hoxne, is less easy to understand as they comprised mainly undamaged and serviceable household items. Although the bullion may have been hidden for security reasons, the circumstances suggest a continuation of prehistoric votive traditions. It is a paradox that the wealthiest and most Classically educated people in later Roman Britain continued to follow such traditions.

ART IN SOCIETY

As the impetus for using art to demonstrate one's Roman allegiances declined, aristocratic display moved increasingly from the public arena to the private. In the early empire power was emphasized through the construction of urban public buildings. Once the province was integrated art and architecture were increasingly used to emphasize distinctions of rank and wealth within society. The rich invested more in great villas, adorned with mosaic floors and decorated wallplaster exclusively for private display. Their design and decoration defined the different areas used to receive visitors of different status, over-awing social inferiors and impressing equals. They were designed with layouts that emphasized their owner's rank, learning and prestige. Likewise the silver plate that graced their dining-tables was decorated in a Late Antique style (**80**). This not only identified their owners with people of similar class across the empire, but also distinguished them from their poorer countrymen who were insufficiently educated to understand the mythology and symbols depicted. Symbols and displays of wealth separated the rich and powerful from the ordinary people. By the fourth century the accumulation of wealth meant that aristocrats in Britain had more in common with similar people in Gaul or Africa than with the peasants on their estates. This change from an ethnically differentiated society to one that divided people by class is at its most evident through the arts.

As the native peoples used artistic symbols from the Roman world in a variety of ways so too did the Roman army. Soldiers and officers who crossed the Channel at the time of the invasion were important in introducing a new range of objects. As the frontier of Britain ossified during the middle years of the occupation the army was increasingly engaged on building installations such as forts and frontier works. Soldiers provided both the building labour and the sculptors for these projects, which included elaborate buildings. This created strong stylistic affinities between the various British forts and those in other parts of the empire.

Military influence is also clear from large numbers of sculptured and inscribed stones found on the frontiers. Many were produced by local craft-workers for military patrons although some may have been made by soldiers themselves. The inscribed stones illustrate the highly Romanized tastes of the soldiers although by the end of the first century the bulk of the army was locally recruited. Their maintenance of Classical traditions consciously expressed the soldiers' membership of a Roman culture.

78 *(right)* Drawing of the fourth-century mosaic pavement from the villa at Hinton St Mary, Dorset. The lower half of the pavement contains a central roundel with a male figure with the Christian chi-rho monogram behind. This may be a portrait of Christ, although the Christian monogram could simply have been used because of its association with the emperor. The figures in the corners have been interpreted as personifications of the winds. In the upper part of the mosaic the central roundel shows Bellerophon slaying the Chimaera, which some have argued was an allegory for the Christian triumph of good over evil (drawn by David S. Neal).

79 *(below)* Nineteenth-century illustration showing the head of summer from the seasons' mosaic found at Dyer Street in Cirencester in 1849. The stylized head combines the simple use of colour with abstract shape to provide a good synthesis of Celtic and Classical art. This pavement is usually dated to the late second to early third century on stylistic grounds.

The purchasing power of the soldiers also brought greater access to Roman objects than in civilian sites nearby. Sites on the frontier are very rich in small objects such as jewellery. Few of these can be considered artistic, but their sheer numbers define a culture that basked in personal display both within and outside the camp. Similar fashions of personal dress spread through the Romanized parts of the civilian zone. Some items of military regalia such as brooches and belt-fittings even came to signify authority and were thus later adopted by Germanic peoples (**81, 105**). Many of the most intricate items, such as engraved intaglios illustrating Classical themes, are found concentrated at military sites where Classical taste evidently remained dominant.

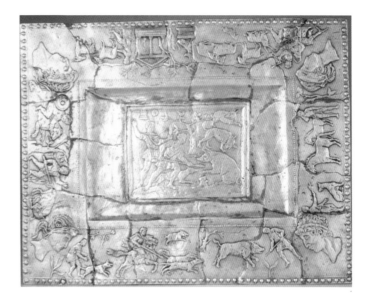

80 *(right)* The Risley Park lanx, or silver tray. Silver plate was commonly used in the later Roman world but details of the workmanship of this piece suggest that it was manufactured in Britain. The decoration shows hunting scenes typical of the aristocratic lifestyle of the period. On the underside of this piece there is an inscription which reads in translation: 'Bishop Exuperius gave this to the Bogiensian church' followed by a chi-rho symbol. The lanx was no doubt given as part of an endowment, illustrating how ordinary objects, even those with pagan symbolism, might have come into the possession of the Church.

81 *(below)* Three fourth-century crossbow brooches found in graves to the east of London. Such brooches were essentially functional safety-pins used to fasten a cloak at the shoulder. However, during the later empire some of these brooches were used as official insignia, or badges of office, by both civil servants and soldiers.

The failure of Roman styles to be adopted beyond the frontiers, and the survival of Celtic styles there, suggest a rejection of the symbols of an alien culture. Hostile frontiers are often marked by sharp cultural and linguistic distinctions as symbols are used to stress differences between neighbours. The wide availability of Roman objects in frontier areas and their general scarcity in adjacent regions imply that natives outside the frontier often rejected Roman styles in the same way that they rebuffed Roman power. Distinctions between military and civilian sites in frontier areas perhaps suggest a similar social alienation induced by the prolonged military presence.

A rejection of Roman styles of art and architecture is seen across the whole of the former province after the fifth century. Britain saw a complete loss of the Roman architectural and artistic styles. The material that replaced it was entirely Germanic, its architecture no longer monumental and wood was used in place of stone (see **64**). There is little evidence for even the prolongation of Roman styles in the areas that passed to the Saxons after a long period of sub-Roman rule. The wholesale adoption of Germanic tastes thus appears similar to the earlier spread of Roman culture. The styles brought by the incomers were adopted by the indigenous peoples. Thus the arts of the new ascendant power were used by Britons in the same way as they had once taken up the symbols of Roman cultural dominance. Chameleon-like, Britons thus turned from being provincial Romans to become Germanic.

5 THE GODS: RITUALS OF LIFE AND DEATH

THE GODS OF LIFE

Most of our information about religion concerns not what people believed but their rituals and actions. 'Ritual' has too often been used to describe archaeological evidence that is difficult to understand on the assumption that there is a distinction between the rational, functional secular world and irrational, non-functional religious acts. This distinction is not universal and many societies understand different aspects of the world to share both a religious and secular rationale. Establishing a temple at a place where lightning struck the ground has an obvious rationality provided you know the history of the place. Sacrificing an animal on an altar to ensure a successful crop is also easy to understand. It is far more difficult to envisage motives for burying an ox's head beneath the threshold of a building or disposing of a gold hoard in a pit. Neither motive nor rationale is very obvious, and the action may appear bizarre. However, we should not try to separate such actions from those of everyday life and label them as either functional or religious. We may never know what such behaviour meant but if identified repeatedly it was surely significant. Once recognized, rituals can be discussed on the assumption that for most people gods and the powers of nature were always present and controlled the world. They were as real as the rainfall on which lives were equally dependent.

In Iron Age Britain it is difficult to identify anything unambiguously religious since religion was everywhere. For instance, house doors almost invariably faced to the southeast whatever the lie of the land, suggesting they were positioned as a result of social conventions or beliefs. Precious objects were commonly deposited in rivers and bogs probably as votive offerings. The burial of pieces of human bodies in disused corn-storage pits was also a ritual perhaps associated with fertility and the harvest, while objects like iron currency bars were often buried at boundaries. In the same way, the burial of very large numbers of gold torcs in pits at Snettisham in Norfolk was clearly deliberate and arguably votive (**83**).

Such spectacular patterns are the tip of an iceberg, for on ordinary domestic sites burials of items like animal heads or complete pottery vessels were common. Even the disposal of domestic refuse was sometimes very carefully organized. Analysis of

82 *(right)* The body of a man deposited in the peat bog at Lindow Moss, Cheshire, between 2 BC and AD 119. He appears to have been an aristocrat who was sacrificed before being placed in the bog. The find of his body was exceptional, but there is a pattern of religious finds associated with wet places in both Iron Age and Roman Britain.

the finds from settlements in southern England has shown how different parts of the site were used exclusively for particular kinds of rubbish with obvious distinctions, for instance, between bones of various animal species. Equally, there is now substantial evidence that some animal burials represent religious offerings (**84**). Likewise the relatively commonplace discovery of isolated Iron Age gold coins indicates purposeful deposition rather than accidental losses, especially as many are found close to water. Although the reasons for deposition remain obscure there is little doubt that the ritual was meaningful to the people involved. The items that have survived are not necessarily typical, as organic materials, for example ears of corn, may have been particularly important within agrarian communities.

Exceptionally we glimpse details of a particular event. The bog body found at Lindow Moss in Cheshire in 1984 provides an excellent example (**82**). Deposited between 2 BC and AD 119, the body was of a man in his late twenties, naked except for a fox-fur armband. His well-manicured fingernails show he was an aristocrat. Burial in these remote wetlands followed death as a sacrifice. Examination of his well-preserved body shows that he had been asphyxiated with a garrotte, hit over the head and had his throat cut, before being thrown into the marsh. He might also have eaten a ritual meal of cereal griddle cakes before going to his death. The information from this find is exceptional although other bog bodies have been found.

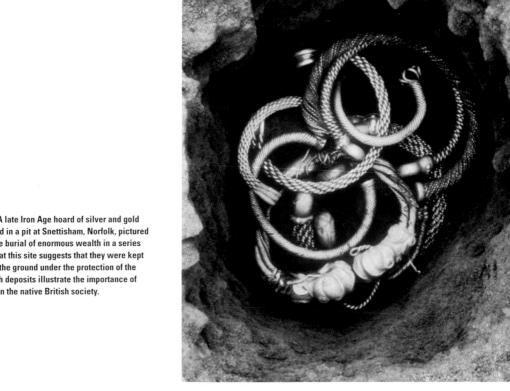

83 *(right)* A late Iron Age hoard of silver and gold torcs found in a pit at Snettisham, Norfolk, pictured *in situ*. The burial of enormous wealth in a series of hoards at this site suggests that they were kept hidden in the ground under the protection of the gods. Such deposits illustrate the importance of hoarding in the native British society.

THE EMERGENCE OF TEMPLES

Archaeological evidence of Iron Age ritual comes from a variety of places and there is scant evidence that it was focused on specially constructed temples, although particular locations like the river Thames or the area that contained the Snettisham hoards did attract unusual attention. If gods were thought to be everywhere we might ask why some places were more appropriate for veneration than others. Roman writers mention that Celts worshipped in isolated places, such as sacred woodland groves, and some localities where ritual deposits are found may have been such sanctuaries without buildings.

In recent years careful excavation at a few Roman temples has revealed Late Iron Age precursors. These sites were in southeastern England close to Gaul and all date to the period when close contacts were developing. One of the best known lay on Hayling Island in Hampshire and consisted of a simple round wooden building set in a square enclosure. It was identical with many ordinary houses and is identified as a temple because of the later temple superimposed on it and the rich votive deposits of coins, weapons and meat bones from the surrounding courtyard. These show strong parallels with sites across the Channel where temples already existed. The idea of temple building was thus apparently brought in from Gaul with the other elite fashions in the period leading up to the conquest of AD 43.

Similarities between the Hayling temple and an ordinary house suggest that the choice was deliberate. Given the presence of gods everywhere in ordinary life it was perhaps appropriate for a deity to be housed like any other important member of the community.

84 *(right)* Careful burial of a calf in wet ground at Shiptonthorpe, East Yorkshire. On this site, a water-hole became the focus for the burial of human infants and young animals, suggesting that both were votive offerings. Such patterns of behaviour, which originate in the Iron Age, demonstrate how native religious practice continued through the Roman period.

Alternatively the temple may have originated as the home of a revered individual. Perhaps a hero, who became a god on his or her death. Hayling would not have been identified as a temple without either votive deposits or the later temple on top. This raises the question of how many other Iron Age houses acted as homes for gods. A number of earlier Iron Age buildings, rectangular structures at the centres of hill-forts for instance, are sometimes seen as shrines although none has yet produced evidence to support their identification as special religious buildings. This does not mean that they did not house gods; it simply highlights the ambiguities discussed.

The development of specialized places of worship has profound implications, suggesting the beginning of a clear separation of religion from other aspects of life. Temple building did not come directly from the Mediterranean since the first temples were built in a Romano-Celtic style (**85**). This was widespread within north-western Europe and became common in the civilian areas of Britain during the early Roman period. Romano-Celtic temples normally consisted of a square or rectangular central building (the *cella*) surrounded by a concentric wall that created a passage or ambulatory. It stood within a sacred enclosure, or *temenos*. Such temples were not for congregational worship but acted as shrines to house gods, represented by cult images or other manifestations such as sacred trees. Variations in the design were presumably determined by the character of the gods worshipped. Religious ceremonial took place largely within the *temenos* where votive deposits were often carefully buried.

These patterns of use were similar to those of the Classical world where a sacrificial altar stood in front of the temple within the sacred

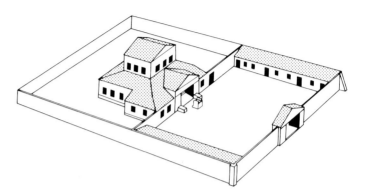

85 *(right)* The Romano-Celtic temple at Harlow, Essex, as it may have appeared around AD 200. The temple itself is typical of its kind with a central shrine, or cella, surrounded by a roofed gallery. This was set within the sacred enclosure, or *temenos*, within which the ceremonials took place. The altar is seen in front of the main entrance. Temples such as this were widely distributed across Britain (see **89**) and the western provinces of the empire. They represent the Romanization of one aspect of native religious practice and were similar in function and layout to Classical temples whose designs derived from the Mediterranean (see **75**).

enclosure (see **75**). This is no coincidence since Romano-Celtic temples evolved from a fusion of Classical and Celtic influences. The introduction of this style of temple to Britain via Gaul before the Roman invasion was thus a secondary effect of Roman expansion. The religions of Romans and Celts were thus sufficiently similar in liturgy to allow such a cross-fertilization of ideas.

ROMAN ATTITUDES TO RELIGION

The army of invasion brought with it new patterns of worship and stimulated changes in native religion. Roman attitudes towards the religions of their conquered peoples were fairly straightforward. They conceived of the world as inhabited by a wide range of different gods to whom it was appropriate to pay respect. There was no concept that their religion took precedence over that of others and all gods were to be seen side by side. The acceptance of local gods was quite normal, for the Romans worshipped native gods in their own ways. The only exceptions were those religions that claimed exclusivity and thus denied the legitimacy of the Roman gods. Some of these also acted as foci for anti-Roman sentiment and so became objects of Roman repression. This provides the context for understanding Roman attitudes to Judaism and Christianity. The Romans also detested ceremonies that involved human sacrifice, although they themselves had only recently abandoned it and continued with the rituals of gladiatorial combat.

In Britain the only known conflict with the Druids was on the Island of Mona (Anglesey). This was a centre of resistance to Rome and was attacked both in AD 60 and 78. Tacitus vividly described their resistance with both cursing Druids and women dressed in black like Furies. He mentions the pouring of human blood on altars and the inspection of human entrails but these are the only direct evidence for human sacrifice and Druids in Roman Britain. The term 'Druid' unfortunately conjures up contemporary images of people in long robes dancing around Stonehenge at midsummer. Modern Druids are a nineteenth-century re-creation of a romanticized past and bear no resemblance to the first-century defenders of Anglesey.

The little literary information about the Druids refers to Gaul. Here the Druids were apparently not a religious sect but a priestly class of high social rank. Status was probably derived from their learning and their keeping of the laws and traditions. Their role was more than simply religious. The island was clearly an important centre for Iron Age peoples, perhaps a sanctuary where meetings between tribes took place and conflicts were resolved under the protection of the gods. As respected elders, lawmakers and protectors of traditions the Druids were involved in resistance to Rome. For the Romans their religion was of less importance than the active role that the sanctuary played in resistance. The suppression of the Druids was thus not a product of religious intolerance but *realpolitik*.

ROMAN RELIGIOUS PRACTICES

Following the invasion, Roman religious practices arrived together with those which blended the Classical and Celtic. Some resulted from an integration of the two traditions within Britain, but others were imported from Europe where the fusion had already been forged. As new patterns of worship emerged, native traditions also continued. However, the Romanization of these practices gradually made them more visible to archaeologists.

Romanized administrators presumably introduced the worship of the principal Roman state gods, the Capitoline triad of Jupiter, Juno and Minerva, to centres like London. Their worship would be expected in *coloniae* and other places populated with Roman citizens. The only definite evidence for their worship comes in the form of dedications to Jupiter Optimus Maximus, which were not concentrated at particular towns. Incomers were also responsible for the establishment at Colchester of the great Classical temple dedicated to the deified emperor Claudius, built to provide a provincial cult centre for the new province. Its dedication to the deified emperor illustrates how the Romans associated human and divine power. The deification of emperors provided an important focus for loyalty in the conquered territories and their divine power was called upon to justify and support political control. The

86 *(right)* Sculpture on an inscription slab from Bridgeness, West Lothian, showing an officer of the Second Legion Augusta pouring a libation over an altar while pipes play to drown out sounds of ill-omen. Beside the altar are the three animals to be sacrificed to Mars. This particular ceremony was probably the *suovetaurilia*, a ritual cleansing in preparation for crossing the boundary into barbarian territory. The general form of the ceremony is typical of Roman religion and shows how altars were used.

magnificent temple at Colchester served as a symbol for Roman control of Britain and struck awe into the hearts of those who came to appreciate the power of the empire through it (see **43**). The imperial cult was not only worshipped at Colchester; there is also evidence for it at London, York and Lincoln.

The emperor's power was an important focus for army loyalty and religious evidence from fort sites provides ample evidence for the worship of the imperial household, the spirits of the emperors and individual leaders. For soldiers, as for everyone else, the year was punctuated by regular religious festivals of considerable importance for a society without weekends. On each festival day an appropriate sacrifice was made at an altar by the commanding officer (**86, 87**). The slaughtered animal was opened up and its liver inspected so that the priest could read the omens. Animals were usually barbecued and eaten communally as part of the festival. The debris was subsequently

87 *(above)* Stone altar similar to that shown on the Bridgeness slab (86). This particular example was found at Eastgate in Co. Durham, distant from any known Roman settlement. It is appropriately dedicated to Silvanus, god of the woods. In translation it reads: 'To the god Silvanus. Aurelius Quirinus, prefect, made this.'

88 *(above right)* Map showing the distribution of inscribed altars from Roman Britain. The main concentrations are found in areas long occupied by the army.

carefully disposed of within the religious precinct. These rituals helped reinforce social cohesion and maintain social hierarchies. In addition to the range of Roman deities worshipped, the army on the frontiers adopted local gods, which they worshipped in similar ways.

Such rituals are easier to detect than the earlier Celtic practices because they resulted in the erection of both inscriptions and sculptured images. Many altars were inscribed, and recorded not only the names of gods and those who made dedications, but also formulaic abbreviations which reveal their purposes such as the fulfilment of an earlier vow. They also provide information about those making dedications (see **71**). The tradition of recording acts of worship in permanent inscriptions and producing sculptures of gods in human form were alien to the indigenous people but spread widely through the province. Their distribution was, however, largely limited to particular regions and did not permeate all ranks

89 *(right)* Map showing the distribution of Romano-Celtic temples in Roman Britain. These are mainly found in the areas that were under civilian administration and are rare in those areas where the army were based.

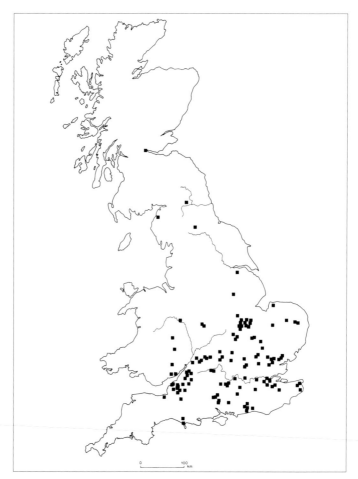

of society. Although many were dedicated to native gods, altars have rarely been found at Romano-Celtic temples (**88, 89**). They are found in greater numbers at Classical temples, like Bath, which were evidently frequented by soldiers and officials from outside the province. They were also common at forts and the more cosmopolitan towns like London. Few Classical temples are known in Britain and these were on the frontier or at the more important towns. This demonstrates how more Romanized traditions were mostly favoured by the soldiers and other immigrants.

The distribution of altars was distinct from that of Romano-Celtic temples that were concentrated in the south, Midlands and east, largely away from the military sites. There were thus two broad forms of religious ritual, one characterized by the use of temples, and the other by the dedication of inscribed stone altars. This implies a social distinction between the religious practices of the forts'

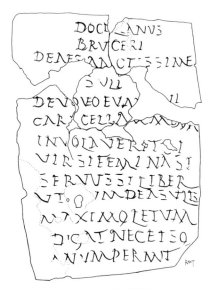

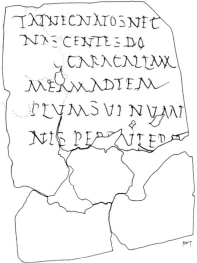

90 *(above) Defixio*, or curse tablet, from the temple of Sulis Minerva at Bath (74, 75). This example reads in translation: 'Docilianus son of Brucerus to the most holy goddess Sulis. I curse him who has stolen my hooded cloak, whether man or woman, whether slave or free. May the goddess Sulis inflict death upon him and not allow him sleep or children now and in the future, until he has brought my hooded cloak to the temple of her divinity.'

occupants and those who worshipped at the temples. Sculptural representations of the gods were more widely used than inscriptions.

Important information about the religion practised at temple sites has been provided by excavations at Bath and Uley in Gloucestershire where large collections of small lead tablets bearing inscriptions have been found within the sacred precincts. These curse tablets *(defixiones)* were letters addressed to the gods that provide insights into people's expectations for divine intervention (**90**). Most were written in a longhand on to the lead. They are extremely difficult to decipher, especially as some were written backwards and most had been rolled up before deposition. They have a formulaic character: they begin by addressing the god, outline the worshipper's request, then often ask for a wrong to be righted or avenged. They then specify who might be to blame, but since it was essential to provide correct information many contained open descriptions of culprits. 'Whether man or woman, slave or free.' These texts resemble Roman contracts and owe more to Rome than native traditions. Comparative examples come from across the empire, including the Greek world, suggesting that the practice of addressing deities in this way was a Classical import. It is doubtful whether they were typical of the ordinary Britons, and worship at the shrines may have been rather socially exclusive. Despite isolated finds from a few other temples it would be unwise to use *defixiones* to generalize about religious practices over the whole province.

Religion in Britain was also characterized by the habit of twinning native gods' names with those from the Classical world. The temple at Bath was dedicated to the goddess Sulis Minerva. Such naming is usually referred to by the term *interpretatio Romana*, but it is not easy to understand. Tacitus tells us that a Germanic tribe outside the empire worshipped a pair of gods they called Alci whom he says 'were called Castor and Pollux in the Roman interpretation'. This resulted from Roman openness to the beliefs of others. The pairing of names shows that native gods shared sufficient characteristics with a Roman deity to allow them to be equated. Rather than just calling the native god by the name of its Roman equivalent, both names were used. The gods were thus thought of ambiguously, being both synonymous and distinct. This surely indicated a hazy understanding entirely appropriate for those trying to grasp the otherness of the divine world. In the case of Bath the goddess perhaps had general characteristics that identified her with the Classical Minerva although she retained a separate identity, Sulis, unique and particular to her mysterious hot-water spring. Most inscriptions were dedicated by immigrants and the more Romanized population, so double-naming was also a product of this social group. Those new to a province were perhaps best able to reconcile themselves to its unfamiliarity through this identification of local gods with their own. Most dedications in frontier areas used only a native god's name. Such gods are mostly known from only one or two dedications, although a few, such as Epona, were more widespread and are also found outside Britain. Some were distributed in limited regions implying that they characterized a particular place and a few, such as Brigantia, bore the names of individual tribes. Other localized deities are indicated by the limited distributions of sculptures depicting unnamed gods.

CONTINUITY OF NATIVE PRACTICES

This evidence of change in religious expressions obscures the continuity of some Iron Age cult practices and the development of local cult activities within Roman Britain, which, although widespread, are much less obvious and are not fully understood. The careful burial of animals in ritual contexts and the deposition of objects in wet places continued but came to include Roman items like arms and sculpture. This evidence has been given less prominence than the more formalized and obviously religious evidence of temples and altars. Excavations at Shiptonthorpe in East Yorkshire examined a communal animal watering-place at the centre of a roadside village. The water-hole went out of use and included in its backfill were carefully placed whole pots, an ox's head and a pair of dogs' skulls. The pond was then used as a burial place for young animals and human babies (84). The meaning of these practices is not clear but the evidence suggests a ritual associated with a water deity. Similar associations between unusual deposits and water are not uncommon. Several wells in Hampshire contained animals, including cockerels, and sets of complete pots. Similarly, hoards of late Roman pewter vessels were often hidden in wells, perhaps suggesting that they too were votive offerings. These examples also demonstrate how indigenous practices were modified by the use of Roman objects. Their widespread occurrence shows

91 *(right)* Three clay statuettes of Venus found in the eastern cemetery of Roman London, dated to the second century AD. These mass-produced religious objects were imported from Gaul and seem to represent the popular adoption of this classical goddess in Roman Britain.

92 *(below)* Bronze head from a statue of the Emperor Hadrian found in the Thames at London. It may simply have been thrown in the river after having been cut from the torso. But, it could also have been deposited deliberately since there is widespread evidence for both the veneration of the head and the ritual deposition of items in wet places in Roman Britain.

how such rituals developed alongside formal Romanized religion and were presumably practised more by ordinary people. It confirms the Elder Pliny's assertion in the first century AD that magic was widespread in Britain.

One of the more subtle ways in which Romanization affected the native population was through a burgeoning use of small religious objects. These are found widely on both the military and civilian sites. Some, such as the small clay figures of gods, are relatively easy to comprehend as images of either newly introduced deities, like Venus, or traditional ones, like the mother goddesses (**91**). There was also a range of more ambiguous objects that illustrate the rites and ceremonies of ordinary people. Some may have superseded Iron Age images made from materials such as wood, although a growth in the use of icons clearly accompanied Romanization.

One widely represented tradition was the veneration of the human head. The collection of human heads was evidently limited, although literary sources document the practice in Gaul at an earlier date. A collection of skulls from the Walbrook stream in London confirms that human heads were ritually deposited in rivers along with items of display metalwork. From this developed the use of sculptured stone heads, and the discovery of heads from Roman bronze sculptures in rivers illustrates the Romanization of the practice (**92**).

Smaller ritual objects included a wide range of spoked wheels thought to have symbolized the sun, moon and seasons. A similar preoccupation can be identified in sculptures that show the sun and moon either realistically or with wheel symbols. Another very widespread image was fertility in the form of the mother goddess. A wide range of other deities are also known including goddesses such as Venus and gods of war, often Mars, who was especially venerated within the army. Equally, there were a relatively large number of phallic symbols, which derived from Mediterranean traditions where they were widely used as talismans. Their adoption here also illustrates the spread of Roman popular traditions although their combination with symbols such as heads suggests integration with Celtic practices.

The continued association of wet places with rituals was developed within the Roman tradition with the veneration of places like the hot spring at Bath and the well dedicated to Coventina at Carrawburgh on Hadrian's Wall. At Bath, healing was connected with the shrine; for example an ivory model breast was found in the spring. Symbolism from elsewhere was also related to medicine, with items like the small metal votive plaques shaped as eyes found at Wroxeter. Such models of different parts of the human body were presumably used as offerings to encourage the healing of particular organs. They were neither exclusively Celtic nor Roman, but had a widespread distribution across the whole empire. Models of animals and birds, both domesticated and wild, are also found. Their significance is less certain, although many were apparently religious. Some may have been beasts associated with natural deities but others, such as the cattle drawing a plough found at Piercebridge, probably celebrated the Roman practice of ploughing to define the territory of a settlement (see **35**).

Such small items were perhaps associated with household shrines, several of which have been excavated. Most notable was that in a cellar at the Lullingstone villa in Kent where a pair of marble portrait busts together with two votive pots derived from a shrine. These were probably dedicated to ancestors as was common in Roman tradition. Other smaller objects were portable charms. Some may have been obtained at major shrines for ceremonial deposition or as keepsakes. Whatever their use these durable pieces provide wide indications of belief and daily religious practice.

The coexistence of Roman public cults with indigenous religion raises the question of why native religion changed in character. Religion was an expression of social values as well as fulfilling deeper needs, so the adoption of Romanized forms at first expressed the aspirations of tribal aristocrats to be Roman. As social leaders also acted as priests in many cults, their views presumably had an important influence on how indigenous rituals changed following contact with Rome. In this sense religion mirrors other aspects of Romanization. Participation in Roman religious rituals was also significant in the process by which ambitious natives adopted Roman values for it implied a deeper sympathy with and understanding of Roman ideas. Changes in native religious practice also provide clear evidence for the thorough merging of native and Roman ideas.

NEW CULTS OF THE LATER EMPIRE

Some more Romanized public towns and forts also provide evidence for minority adherence to cults that originated from the eastern empire, most typically in the middle years of Roman rule. Mithras was worshipped at several temples, the best known being in London. Membership of such Oriental cults was limited to those initiated into the mysteries of the religion. Their buildings were used for congregational worship unlike those of Roman or Romano-Celtic religions. Excavated *Mithraea* were semi-subterranean halls in which secret ceremonies took place with the participants hidden from outsiders.

These cults and similar religious guilds were socially exclusive and attracted rich and powerful adherents. High quality, often imported, works of art are associated with their worship (**93**). Although such cults were never popular, their worshippers were influential and linked initiates in Britain with those in other parts of the empire through what was effectively an exclusive secret society. Their occurrence provides further evidence for the integration of the nobility with those in the mainstream of Roman power.

Eastern cults were spread by soldiers and administrators and are said to have fulfilled deep psychological needs not met by the apparently hollow ceremonials of the public religions. Christianity shared many characteristics with the other Eastern cults. It probably arrived through the same routes and perhaps fulfilled similar personal needs among its converts. Christianity spread widely through the cities of the empire soon after its establishment, but distinctive architectural or archaeological characteristics did not develop until

93 *(right)* Marble relief from the temple of Mithras in London showing the bull-slaying that was central to the Mithraic religion. The surroundings of the scene show the sun (upper left) and moon (upper right) being carried across the sky, with two heads of the winds below, while the circular frame contains symbols of the zodiac. Mystery cults like this one were frequented by cosmopolitan officials and the military. In translation the inscription reads: 'Ulpius Silvanus, re-enlisted retired soldier of the Second Legion Augusta, paid his vow. Enlisted at Orange [in southern Gaul].'

the fourth century. Early Christian groups met in private rooms that, although acting as places of congregational worship, were not architecturally distinctive. Since Christianity periodically attracted the adverse attentions of government it developed no unambiguous artistic symbols. Those used could generally be read in at least two ways. This makes it exceptionally difficult to identify evidence of early Christianity. In Britain, private house churches are known at a few villas, and were perhaps originally more widespread. Wall paintings of the early fourth century from a room at the Lullingstone villa show a person in the traditional early Christian attitude of prayer with their arms outstretched, implying that this room was used for Christian worship. The mid-fourth-century mosaic from a reception room in the villa at Hinton St Mary in Dorset depicts a head that may be Christ, so it is often assumed that the house had a Christian owner (see **78**). These and other sites illustrate the presence of Christianity in private houses but none is dated to before the fourth century. That Christians were known is illustrated by one of the Bath curses that cites a culprit 'whether pagan or Christian'.

Christianity before the fourth century is evidenced by historical sources which record the martyrdom of three Christians, presumably members of a larger community. St Alban was put to death at Verulamium in the third century, while Aaron and Julius died at Caerleon probably during one of the third-century persecutions. We simply do not know how many other believers there were but there is little reason to suspect that it was more than a thinly spread minority cult like the other new religions of the period.

94 *(right)* Bezel of a jet finger-ring showing the chi-rho symbol used by early Christians. This ring came from the fill of a grave excavated at Bagshot, Surrey, in 1993. It is a good example of the type of portable object on which early Christian symbols were often inscribed. The form of the lettering suggests a date in the second half of the fourth century AD.

Christianity changed radically after the conversion of the Emperor Constantine, who saw a vision before his victory at the battle of Milvian Bridge in 312. His personal experience led him to accept Christianity as one of the religions of the empire, although it did not become the official state religion replacing the pagan cults until 391. Constantine's acceptance of it allowed Christian worship to be practised publicly, and provided a respite from periodic persecutions.

The effects of its recognition are not easy to assess in Britain. Historical sources tell us that Christian bishops from York, Lincoln and London attended a church council at Arles in 314. New-found respectability also encouraged a growth of Christianity, especially among the more influential members of society influenced by the emperor. Elsewhere in the empire luminaries like Helena, the emperor's mother, became active supporters, endowing new churches.

Given an upsurge in support and the increasing visibility of congregations, it would not be surprising if Christianity had become more widespread in Britain. Identifiable symbols (**94**) and spectacular Christian objects are relatively common but we have comparatively little evidence of church buildings (**95**). There is very little evidence that large churches were built although this partly results from difficulties in their recognition. The growth of Christian worship led to the adoption of building forms borrowed from the repertoire of Roman public architecture and only later in the fourth and fifth centuries did distinctive styles evolve. The building types most commonly adopted were the basilica and large halls (similar to those used in public baths) with occasional centrally planned structures similar to mausolea used at shrines.

The key requirement was that congregations could meet indoors, so the basilica was the most widespread and appropriate form. Unfortunately this makes churches almost impossible to distinguish from similar secular structures or buildings used as pagan guild meeting-places. A number of possible churches has been identified, the most plausible of which have baptismal fonts standing in front of them. In the early Christian churches only the baptized were admitted, so baptistries were often built outside,

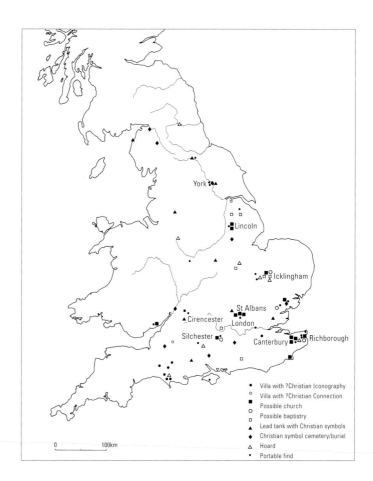

95 *(right)* Map of Britain showing the distribution of the evidence for Christianity. The general spread is similar to that of other traits associated with the Romanization of the civilian population.

usually at the west end of the church. A hall-shaped building at the fort of Richborough in Kent with a font in front was probably a church (see **60**). A similar font stood outside a small building in the centre of Silchester (**96**). However, its plan is unparalleled elsewhere in the fourth century and doubts remain about whether it was a church rather than the meeting-house of another cult. The necessity of baptism does not allow us to dismiss buildings without an identifiable font. A number of lead tanks have also been discovered with Christian monograms on them, which appear to have been fonts that stood on the ground surface without leaving any trace. Given these problems we can only guess at the extent of Christian worship in late Roman Britain.

In addition to ordinary congregational churches, shrines were constructed over graves of early Christian fathers and martyrs. Most notable were those of the apostles in Rome. These early Christians had been buried in ordinary town cemeteries. Their tombs were

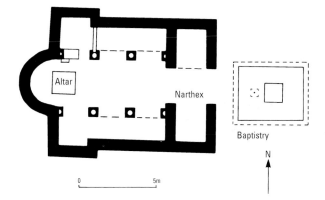

96 *(right)* Plan of the possible fourth-century church from beside the forum at Silchester. The general shape of the plan and the presence of a separate baptistry support its identification as a church, but as transepts would be unusual at this date and it is very small, this is by no means certain. If not a church, it may have been a meeting-place for another cult.

subsequently venerated but it was only with the official recognition of Christianity that shrines were constructed.

British martyrs' burials might be expected to have led to the construction of similar churches. This almost certainly happened at St Albans across the river from Roman Verulamium. This shrine of St Alban is mentioned in Constantius' account of St Germanus' visit to Britain in 429 although we have no archaeological evidence for the precise location of either grave or Roman church. Possible Roman churches have been found over earlier graveyards and these hint at the burials of otherwise unknown martyrs. Best surviving is the small, possibly Roman, square structure built into the core of the Saxon church at Stone-by-Faversham in Kent, beside the cemetery of the Roman roadside settlement of Ospringe. The incorporation of similar Roman martyria into medieval churches was commonplace on the Continent, but in Britain the pagan Saxon interlude generally broke any such continuity.

If the evidence for Christian structures is patchy and ambiguous there is a far more impressive array of portable finds illustrating the importance of the religion in fourth-century Britain (**95**). Most notable are the finds of silver plate such as the treasure from Water Newton in Cambridgeshire (**97**) and the tray rediscovered in 1991 from Risley Park in Derbyshire. The latter has a chequered history having been recast and lost after its original discovery in 1729 (see **80**). It is decorated with hunting and pastoral scenes that have no apparent Christian associations. However, an inscription on its underside reads 'Bishop Exuperius gave this to the Bogiensian church'. The location of this church is unknown but, as it was probably manufactured in Britain, the congregation to whom it was presented was also presumably here.

The most spectacular Christian find was the treasure discovered at the Roman small town of Water Newton (Durobrivae) near

97 *(above)* The hoard of early Christian silver plate found at Water Newton (Durobrivae), Peterborough. The objects probably date to the middle of the fourth century AD and, as such, represent the earliest known set of church plate. The Church acquired such plate through gift (80), and this accounts for the rather diverse make-up of the treasure.

Peterborough. This comprised 28 silver objects probably deposited in the late fourth century (**97**). There were a jug, bowls, cups and silver plaques plus a wine strainer and a single gold disc. The plaques are of a triangular, leaf-like shape often associated with pagan temples, although some of the Water Newton examples bear the Christian chi-rho monogram, illustrating how Christianity adopted pagan forms of votive objects. Three of the larger pieces carry Christian inscriptions and apparently record the donation of the objects to the church. The whole treasure is best interpreted as church plate, which presumably belonged to a congregation at the town.

Pieces from several other late Roman silver hoards may also be associated with Christianity. This is suggested by the presence in them of spoons bearing Christian inscriptions and monograms, which may have been used for Communion. Likewise wine strainers from the Thetford treasure may have been used for the Mass, although other items in that treasure have definite associations with the pagan Roman cult of Faunus. This ambiguous mixture of items associated with the worship of different cults should not concern us for objects in such treasures ultimately derived from different sources. The Risley Park lanx illustrates that pagan-style objects came into the possession of churches, presumably as gifts from rich converts. Christian objects may equally have been acquired by pagan temple treasuries.

The wealth represented by these treasures shows how the rich and powerful were able to endow religious communities in the late Roman world. The church grew rich through such means but these gifts also provide important insights into how such substantial donations emphasized the giver's power and social superiority since the plate was sometimes inscribed by the donor. It is also illustrated by the story of the late Roman heiress Melania, who sold her estates in several provinces including Britain to make benefactions to the church. Such substantial private giving echoes the municipal benefactions that characterized the early empire and fulfilled similar social and political roles.

Interesting issues are also raised by the deposition of these late Roman treasures. They may have been simply deposited for safety in times of trouble but their burial more likely continues the earlier habit of burying rich objects for ritual purposes. We know too little of the context of most treasures to obtain clear insights into the details of their burial, but the Thetford collection came from the edge of an important Late Iron Age and early Roman site, one of the principal power centres of the Icenian tribe. Although long unoccupied, it perhaps remained visible and is likely to have been a place of veneration. These treasures were not necessarily placed as permanent offerings but rather given to the gods for protection in a sacred place, as with the earlier Snettisham hoards (**83**). These great treasures had metropolitan artistic characteristics, showing both pagan mythology and Christian symbolism, and were clearly associated with the aristocracy. It is thus ironic that they came to be buried in acts that continued earlier Celtic traditions.

The quality and magnificence of these objects also provide contrasting insights into the level of acceptance of Christianity. We can never know how many adherents the church had but these objects show that among the believers were rich and powerful members of the community. They were as Christianized and as Classical in their tastes as any in the western empire. They were presumably among the educated classes whom the historical sources show to have engaged in debate on the theological issues that obsessed the intellectual world of the late empire. In these discussions Britons such as Pelagius were the equals of any. Christianity thus illustrates how Romanized Britain had become by the fourth century.

THE PEOPLE IN DEATH

Attitudes to death were undoubtedly influenced by religious beliefs and the rituals of life. Archaeological evidence and inscriptions provide a very broad range of information about the rituals of death. Through no other means can we get so close to an understanding of individual people of the period. Although the information is imperfect and understanding it is not always straightforward, burial provides evidence about physique, about aspects of demography, disease and social organization as well as beliefs about death and afterlife. It is important not to be too naïve in interpretation since anthropologists have shown that burial rites do not always mirror life or the organization of society. The richness of a grave's furnishing sometimes shows that the deceased was a rich person, but alternatively may betray age, marital status, family connections or sometimes even personal poverty. The science of studying human bones is also fraught with difficulties and it is not always easy to be certain even about straightforward things like the age or sex of a particular skeleton, especially if cremated. Few causes of death leave evidence on the bones so a full understanding of mortality patterns and community health is impossible. Even allowing for these problems, burial information has an enormous and largely untapped potential for providing a deeper understanding of Roman Britain.

One characteristic of the pre-Roman Iron Age is the lack of burials in formal cemeteries. A few exceptional areas, like parts of Wales, Cornwall and East Yorkshire, had long traditions of formal burial, but over most of the country cemeteries are simply not known. In settlements human remains are often found in places like disused corn-storage pits. These bodies were only rarely complete, more often pieces of bodies or heads. Individual limbs, or torsos were buried without obvious ceremonial. Studies of these rather gruesome remains have shown that they were an aspect of the ritual deposition already discussed. Like Lindow Man (**82**) or the human skulls recovered from rivers in London, they represent rituals perhaps concerned with fertility and the gods of the underworld. These discoveries stress links between the burial of the dead and the worship of deities but provide little information about most of the general population.

The lack of bodies raises fascinating questions about people's behaviour and attitudes to death. Bodies were perhaps disposed of in ways that have left little archaeological trace. Some may have been left exposed in the open air to be consumed by the agencies of nature. This practice is consistent with the evidence of incomplete bodies that had been left to decompose before burial. Others were possibly buried, but only at a shallow depth and so have been lost through biological degradation. Other plausible possibilities include cremation and the scattering of ashes, or disposal in rivers. Cannibalism cannot be entirely ruled out but the absence of human bones from among food refuse suggests that it was not widespread.

98 *(above)* An early nineteenth-century view of the Late Iron Age and early Roman burial mounds at Bartlow Hills, Essex. They were probably the graves of well-placed native aristocrats, and few statements of their social status can have been as emphatic as these great burial mounds, which were up to 45 m (147 ft) in diameter and stood up to 13.7 m (45 ft) tall.

The failure to find Iron Age cemeteries does not mean that death was marked by an absence of ceremonial. The burials found in East Yorkshire illustrate elaborate rituals with large and rich groups of objects carefully placed with the dead. Detailed studies of these graves show subtle but significant patterns in layout and contents. In female graves objects surrounded the upper parts of the body while in male graves they were placed around the feet. Other rituals often involved activities by the living such as funerary feasts. Ceremonials for the living often have greater social significance than the ways in which bodies were eventually discarded.

During the later Iron Age a new set of burial traditions spread from the Continent to southern and eastern England. The dead were cremated before burial and their ashes placed in a container and accompanied in the grave by a range of everyday artefacts. These are often found in small cemeteries although the largest contained up to several hundred graves. There was variation in the numbers and types of goods included in different graves. The largest and most spectacular contained dozens of objects of the highest quality. These were obviously the burials of the most powerful individuals. Variations between the graves illustrate the development of a society with increasingly obvious social distinctions. The burgeoning of richer graves took place first in areas where other evidence illustrates increasing social stratification (see **37**). Cremation rituals were closely similar to those on the Continent and were evidently imported with other ideas (**100**). The earliest British burials were sometimes very spectacular and a few were placed beneath great earthen burial mounds designed to symbolize the power of the dead (**98, 99**).

Beside the most richly furnished graves there were many more, often in the larger graveyards that were more simply provided, but often with objects of Gallic or Roman origin. One cemetery beside the *oppidum* at St Albans was originally organized into small plots, which probably held the graves of members of the same family or kin group. Each plot was defined by an enclosure ditch and had at

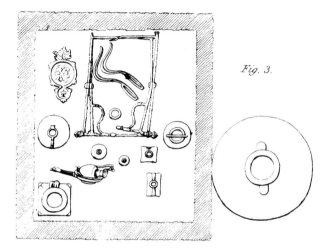

Fig. 3.

99 *(right)* Plan of a grave found beneath the largest burial mound at Bartlow Hills, Essex (98). The cremated body was in a square glass vessel at the bottom left-hand corner. Among the grave-goods was the iron frame of a stool that may have signified kingly status, a bronze lamp, and a collection of glass and bronze vessels from as far afield as Italy. There was also a pair of curved bronze strigils, tools used to scrape sweat from the skin in Roman baths – unusual as the person buried here was unlikely to have had access to a bath-house. They were perhaps kept for their status value. Outside the box was an amphora of olive oil from southern Spain.

its centre a well-furnished grave that was most likely the founder of the group. The other graves in each cluster were similar in layout and contents, and show few obvious distinctions between men and women, or young and old.

The spread of the idea of graves containing items from daily life is often seen as indicating a belief in an afterlife. The provision of grave-furnishings for use in the next world might seem contradictory since cremation itself is difficult to reconcile with a belief in physical rebirth, but objects placed in graves did not necessarily belong to the dead. The rite may be better understood if the objects are seen as gifts from the living designed to symbolize their relationship to the dead. The act of giving at funerals enabled heirs to establish their new social relationships after the death. This may explain the absence of clear distinctions between the graves of people of different age or sex. It also suggests that the range of objects was a result of the scale of a person's social network rather than their individual wealth. A well-known person of high rank received more mourners and thus more funeral gifts. Imported objects, arguably diplomatic gifts, could thus be symbols of a great person's contacts beyond the tribe (**100**).

No immediate change in funerary practice was brought about by the Roman invasion, although cremation burials with grave-goods became more widespread. At major new Roman centres like Colchester burials were increasingly accompanied by additional Gallic objects, such as glass vessels used to contain the ashes of the dead. Cremation also spread beyond the southeast, although many areas remained devoid of cemeteries. From around the time of the conquest there is a series of very impressive burials of native leaders especially in the south and east. They were presumably aristocrats who gained greatly from their support of Rome and whose

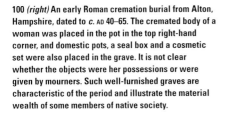

100 *(right)* An early Roman cremation burial from Alton, Hampshire, dated to *c.* AD 40–65. The cremated body of a woman was placed in the pot in the top right-hand corner, and domestic pots, a seal box and a cosmetic set were also placed in the grave. It is not clear whether the objects were her possessions or were given by mourners. Such well-furnished graves are characteristic of the period and illustrate the material wealth of some members of native society.

followers were able to provide them with extremely impressive funerals in the established tradition. In one instance near St Albans a Romano-Celtic temple was constructed beside such a grave about fifty years after the interment. This is of the utmost interest as it shows how the grave continued to be revered long after death.

After an initial period during which impressive burials continued to be very richly furnished, in early Roman graveyards the number and quality of grave-goods tended to decline. Funerals were gradually supplanted for displaying social status by other media such as the construction of town buildings. Moreover the breaking down of traditional family networks, especially in the new urban centres where unrelated people mixed together, perhaps made funerals less important with the attendance of fewer mourners resulting in less objects being deposited.

Another key change came in the location of cemeteries. The Roman tradition of burial exclusively outside the limits of a city was soon adopted, so larger burial grounds were established. These are more easily discovered than the smaller graveyards of the Iron Age. Cemeteries characteristically crowded around the gates and along the approaches to towns. Prestige was evidently gained by having a burial plot and funerary memorial close to the road and as near to the city as possible. However, the magnificent displays of funerary architecture that lined the approaches to towns in other provinces are unknown in Britain, although most major towns had cemeteries around them. Some larger tomb monuments are known from London and other of the major centres but only survive as scraps of sculpture (see **41**).

Inscribed gravestones were most commonly associated with highly Romanized towns and forts (see **41** and **63**). Although a proportion commemorate civilians they were mainly erected for literate immigrants rather than natives. They provide a very good source of information about the person's life and career. Many also give information about age at death and the people who erected the memorials. In Britain most honour members of the army and they are one of the most important sources of information about military garrisons and the distribution of army units. They are similarly informative about the ranks and offices held by civil administrators.

Their value as a source of population data is limited because of the narrow range of people who erected them. Inscribed stone grave-markers were evidently costly and confined to the wealthiest among the population. They also represent a Roman tradition of commemoration, never widely adopted by the natives and which seems to have declined in popularity after the second century. The gravestones rarely record the deaths of children and are biased towards the commemoration of those who died in the prime of life. A notable group records young women who perhaps died in childbirth. A study of these inscriptions provides social insights although they are difficult to generalize from. For the people who erected tombstones, social status measured by a person's origins and career was evidently of great significance. Equally the formulae used on the tombstone inscriptions, which often included either the words 'Here lieth…' or the dedication 'To the gods of the underworld…', betray little detail about people's beliefs beyond demonstrating the adoption of the usual Roman habits. Several epitaphs were dedicated by funerary guilds with which the deceased had deposited money to ensure a proper funeral. They are an important reminder of the importance of memorials for the most Romanized members of society.

From the later second century cremation was progressively replaced by the burial of unburnt corpses, usually laid out on their backs in graves. The significance of this change remains obscure. It is archaeologically important as it makes burials much more visible. Cremation burials deposited in perishable containers like cloth bags unaccompanied by grave-goods are only rarely found simply because they escape notice. They are unlikely to be found casually, for instance during building work.

The better information available for later Roman burial highlights a number of points. The skeletons studied show that the known cemeteries did not contain a representative cross-section of the population. In a living population we know approximately how many people are likely to die within any particular age range. The differing proportions of mortality within age groups reflect the general state of the population. When the cemeteries from Roman Britain are compared with more recent data we find that they fall outside the known ranges, containing too few infants and children. Cemeteries thus contained not the whole population, but usually only the adults. By contrast the bodies of many new-born babies and very young children are found on settlements often in less formal interments. Infants were probably not considered full members of society until they had passed through the first very hazardous months of life. The study of infant burials from some settlement sites has shown that they were only buried in particular locations, suggesting that social rules had to be obeyed. For instance, in the roadside settlement at Shiptonthorpe in East Yorkshire those that died around the time of birth were all carefully placed, buried just outside the walls at the east end of the house.

Further evidence for the selection of who was buried is provided by graveyards excavated in York and Cirencester where there were only small numbers of female graves. This suggests that some burial grounds were segregated by sex. The Cirencester bodies also came from a population with an unusually high proportion of injuries caused by hard manual labour. This predominantly male, peasant cemetery shows how in death as well as in life later Roman Britain witnessed increasing social segregation.

There are also too few burials for the estimated population size. The known cemeteries are largely in the south and east or the frontier areas, so we have no information at all from large parts of the country. Even where we know of cemeteries the total number of burials falls far short of the eighteen or so million people whom we estimate to have lived during the period. Some of the missing dead have undoubtedly been lost through modern destruction; others may one day be excavated. However, there are still vast gaps in our evidence. Most obvious is the general absence of burials from rural areas, which probably accounted for well over 90 per cent of the population.

A few rural burials have been found, typically by the edges of settlements, along field boundaries or beside track ways. Many others may yet be found in similar places under-represented because of their limited chances of accidental discovery. Some rural dead may have been carried to their nearest town for burial in urban cemeteries.

101 *(above)* Vertical aerial photograph showing the layout of the excavated part of the later Roman cemetery at Ashton, Northamptonshire. Extended inhumation burials laid out in orderly rows are characteristic of later Roman cemeteries in Britain and show that the dead were carefully treated.

Despite this there is a genuine shortfall in bodies reminiscent of the Iron Age. Those buried in the graves that we excavate were probably the most Romanized people rather than the majority.

Where excavated, later Roman cemeteries provide a rich source of evidence since they produce both the physical evidence of the bodies and a wide range of grave-goods. In contrast to the earlier cremations a wider variety of burial rite is evident. Different types of object accompanied burials and there were also variations in how and where these were placed in graves. Some distinctions reflect the increasing social hierarchy of the later Roman period. A few graves were distinguished by having funerary buildings, mausolea, constructed over them, which were probably used for ceremonies commemorating the dead. One of these at Poundbury near Dorchester in Dorset was decorated with wall paintings in what may have been a Christian style. Such structures proclaimed the rank and status of the dead person for all to see. Unlike some other parts of the empire there is little evidence for the use of elaborately carved marble coffins that stood in above-ground chambers to be admired by later generations. Some important graves were differentiated by the use of stone coffins or those of lead. The distinction between these burials and those covered by mausolea was that any intention of displaying wealth and status was hidden after the funeral ceremony. At the most basic level most excavated graves contained a range of personal effects and items of clothing. Variations presumably reflected finer social and economic distinctions between those buried.

There was variation not only in the types of objects placed in graves but also where they were laid. In one occasional rite a coin was placed in the mouth of the dead person. This was well known in the Classical world where the coin represented the fee paid to Charon to transport the dead across the river Styx to the underworld. Its discovery in Britain illustrates the adoption of a Classical belief in an afterlife by some of the population. Equally the widespread occurrence of shoes, represented by iron hobnails, at the feet of the dead suggests another version of the same belief in which the dead walked to the afterlife. Differing patterns are identifiable through a study of other objects in the graves. In one of the cemeteries at Lankhills, Winchester most of the bodies had personal possessions placed beside them in the grave while a minority were buried wearing their belts, brooches etc. Such subtle variations are difficult to understand but may reflect regional differences or variations in beliefs, ethnic origins, age, sex or marital status among those buried. In the Lankhills cemetery, the excavator suggested that two particular sets of graves contained continental immigrants who arrived in the second half of the fourth century. This was based on similarities between the styles of burial and grave-goods and those found in cemeteries on the Danube and in the Low Countries. His conclusion may be correct, but we really know too little about the range of burial rites even in southern Britain to be certain that these people, if non-local, did not come from much closer to Winchester. Study of graves like these also shows how it became common in the later Roman world for belts and particular styles of brooch used as military and civil insignia to be deposited in graves (**81, 105**). This presumably meant that they were increasingly important as symbols that defined a person's status and achievements in life, comparable to military uniforms and medals sometimes placed on coffins today.

Grave-goods also provide insights into the distinctions accorded to people of different age and sex. Aside from the tendency for infants not to be accorded formal burial within cemeteries, age differences are not immediately apparent. Although children were usually buried with the same kinds of grave-goods as found with adults, a few examples are known where miniature objects were put in a child's grave. However, detailed study of the occurrence of objects in children's graves at Lankhills, Winchester has shown that social conventions determined what was appropriate to include in the graves of children of different ages. The general pattern confirms that social position and wealth were probably inherited rather than earned anew by each generation. Likewise few obvious distinctions were made between the graves of men and women. Occasional practices distinguished the sexes, for instance later Roman crossbow brooches worn as official insignia were confined to male graves (**81**). The absence of strong gender distinctions lends support to the idea that power within society was monopolized by neither sex.

The treatment of bodies and cemetery layouts also provide information about social values and organization. Most later Roman burials were carefully laid out in regularly cut graves and were buried in either wooden coffins or wrapped in shrouds. Since few of the graves cut into earlier burials, care had obviously been taken and the

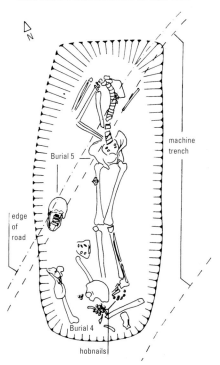

102 *(below)* Plan of a decapitated burial at Cowdery's Down, Basingstoke, Hampshire. The beheading of bodies before burial was a widespread rite in the fourth century, although we cannot be certain why it was done. In this particular instance, the body of one woman (burial 4), which had already decomposed, had been pushed to the foot of the grave before the second decapitated woman (burial 5) was placed there, with her own head beside her right knee.

N

machine trench

Burial 5

edge of road

Burial 4

hobnails

103 *(above)* Later Roman burials from the cemetery to the east of London, buried with gypsum in the coffins. This was in an attempt to preserve the bodies and is a custom that derived from North Africa. The date of its spread across the empire precludes any association with Christianity, and the tradition is probably part of a broader late-Roman trend towards the careful treatment of the dead.

graves marked (**101**). The integrity of dead bodies was presumably held to be significant. As a result, later Roman cemeteries were generally carefully organized with rows of graves oriented either on topographical features, such as an adjacent road, or towards a cardinal point of the compass. Several fourth-century cemeteries were oriented west-east and this has led to the suggestion that they were for Christians. Early Christian communities believed that at the Second Coming people would rise to face their maker, so the dead had to be buried on their backs with their feet to the east. However, the practice of west-east burial does not seem to have been confined to the Christian community as archaeological evidence shows that the fashion had become rooted before the conversion of Constantine.

As obvious care was taken over the laying out of most burials there can be little doubt that exceptions were of significance. Occasional burials in a number of graveyards were placed face down. It is conceivable that this was sometimes accidental, but its frequency suggests a deliberate rite, the meaning of which is by no means clear. If there was a literal belief in rising from the dead those buried in this way may have been people whom the community did not want to return – social outcasts, criminals or other undesirables. An even more curious yet very widespread practice was the decapitation of the dead (**102**). There were several variations in this rite. The head was generally placed by or between the legs, or at the feet, although it is sometimes missing. These burials generally occurred only occasionally in any one cemetery (although in a single graveyard at Dunstable there were a cluster of twelve who had suffered this fate). They might have been criminals or social outcasts but this was certainly not always the case. Infants and children were sometimes decapitated and they are unlikely to have been criminals. Great care was also generally taken over the layout of the graves, suggesting a very formal rite. Medical opinion argues that most beheadings took place after death, implying that the act had a deeper significance. Such attention to heads perhaps results from their veneration in Celtic traditions and the similarities in 'overkill' recall the ritual death of Lindow Man (see **82**). Another late Roman rite appears to have been concerned with preserving bodies in preparation for the afterlife. A widespread but small group of burials was placed in coffins filled with plaster or gypsum (**103**). This was probably intended to preserve the body, and indeed in the

104 *(above)* Plait of hair found in a fourth-century coffin at Dorchester, Dorset. The hair had survived within a lead coffin packed with gypsum (see 103) that held the body of a man aged between 20 and 25 years. The plait was 28 cm (11 in) long and seems to have been cut off using a knife. Long hair was a symbol of potency during the Iron Age, and the discovery of this plait perhaps shows that this tradition continued through the Roman period.

case of one burial from Dorchester it had the effect of preserving a full head of hair (**104**). The rite was apparently introduced from North Africa in the second century and, although there was a possible association with Christianity, it is evident that not all plaster burials were of Christians.

The rise of Christianity in later Roman Britain does seem to have been reflected by changes in cemeteries. The Christian practice of burial without grave-goods, although not consistently adhered to, was reflected in some British cemeteries, as there was a trend towards carefully laid out west-east cemeteries containing unfurnished graves from the fourth century. Such graveyards are, of course, more difficult to date than those that contained a rich array of personal possessions. Some from the west of England, dated by radiocarbon, continued in use from the fourth century into the post-Roman period. It is sometimes argued that the more widespread inclusion of infants and children in fourth-century cemeteries is also a result of the adoption of Christianity. However, a detailed study shows that the proportions of these age groups in cemeteries does not change significantly through the Roman period in Britain.

We will probably never be able to identify Christian cemeteries with certainty, as there was no clear distinction between pagans and Christians. However, the general trends towards unfurnished graves, west-east burial orientation and the sanctity of the grave perhaps provide evidence for the penetration of Christian ideas into later Roman Britain, where they became widespread among the whole of the burying population. As the distinctiveness of burial practices decreased it is very difficult to be certain about the character or precise date of the simple cemeteries characteristic of the West Country in the late Roman and sub-Roman periods. In contrast, in eastern areas of England the spread of Germanic culture brought with it a return to cremation. The dead were buried in simple handmade pottery urns accompanied by new styles of Gothic jewellery. Precisely when this began is still uncertain, but it is unlikely to have been before the first decades of the fifth century. Any Germans in Britain before that date were presumably in the service of Rome and so chose to dress and bury their dead in the local style rather than that of their homelands. As Roman control waned, the population gradually came to adopt the traditions and styles of their new German rulers.

6 THE END OF ROMAN RULE

The decline of Roman power in Britain can only be understood in the context of events elsewhere in the empire. The later Roman period had seen Britain prosper, although increasingly independent from other provinces that were under considerable stress. Administrative reforms had made government more bureaucratic although it still relied on emperors maintaining strong personal control. The empire had been divided into two, each with its own emperor and deputy, thereby generating additional internal stresses. Not only was there rivalry between east and west, but the administrative division made it impossible to direct the resources of the whole empire towards particular problems. The major military problems of the later fourth century were concentrated in the less wealthy western provinces, which thus had to shoulder a heavier financial burden for defence. The army in the west was marginally smaller than that in the east, but contained a larger proportion of the higher-paid field army so it was more costly. The burden of taxation was thus increasingly felt, and many were vocal about it.

Military threats came from tribes beyond the borders, particularly those in Germany who had themselves been affected by migrations from central Asia. This had begun in the third century with invasions that breached the frontier, but by the later fourth the pressures were increasing. Border problems influenced changes in defensive organization, which became increasingly dependent upon a wide network of strongholds (see **61**). These included walled towns as well as forts, such as those around the south and east coast of England (see **10**). At the same time the army experienced recruitment difficulties so drew on manpower from beyond the frontiers. This continued the long-term provincialization of the army as military service offered advancement to those otherwise unable to benefit from the Roman system (**105**).

For Germanic peoples army service gave entry to the Roman world, initially through service in regular units that had enabled individuals to reach the very highest offices. As frontier defence became more difficult, groups of Germans were settled under their own leaders in areas otherwise impossible to defend and were given territory in exchange for their services. There was a gradual breakdown of the frontier as settlers' divided loyalties led them to invite more of their own people to join them. Rome progressively lost territory and this increased the need for her to bribe the

105 *(above)* A late fourth-century, chip-carved belt buckle from a grave in Roman London. Such highly decorative belts were used in the uniforms of members of the Late Roman army, and seem to have signified the rank and status of their owners. The style of decoration was also popular amongst the Germanic peoples who migrated into the Empire at this time, some of them serving in the Roman army. Their adoption of these styles later led to its spread with Germanic settlers.

Germans to hold back. The increased financial burden on the provincial populations fuelled their discontent and provided further opportunities for infiltration. The result was the total loss of the western provinces to barbarian groups by 476. In provinces apart from Britain, incoming Germanic peoples largely took over the Roman infrastructure so that, for instance, the Visigothic kingdom was organized on highly Romanized lines as a result of their desire to join the Roman world.

In Britain the result of the breakdown of Roman control was markedly different and began later. Fourth-century Britain was prosperous in comparison with other parts of the west. Although town walls were elaborated and coastal defences constructed there is little before the 360s to suggest any significant external threat. In 364 and 367–8 Britain was affected by raids that symbolize the beginning of the end although accounts of these raids may be exaggerated.

The events of the later fourth and early fifth centuries are only known in outline, but there was little military pressure on Britain until about 408–10. Britain became a base for successive attempts to wrest control of the troubled western provinces from the legitimate emperor. Usurpers are often said to have weakened Britain's defences by removing troops. There is little evidence to support this and it is more likely that fourth-century Britain was relatively secure and had never contained a large contingent of mobile troops. A crisis came with the Germanic invasion of Italy under Alaric in 401–2, which did result in the withdrawal of troops from Britain. Thus at the beginning of the fifth century Britain was not heavily defended.

The attack on Italy and overrunning of Gaul in 406–7 left Britain as an isolated untroubled area from which came three successive attempts to usurp power. The third pretender, Constantine III, took substantial territories in Gaul and Spain in a successful military campaign. He overcame the barbarians before being defeated by the legitimate emperor, Honorius, in 411. Events in Italy effectively severed Britain's links with Rome. When civic authorities in Britain appealed to Honorius in 410, in the face of Saxon attacks, the emperor told them to look to their own defences. This does not imply any intention of cutting Britain adrift but illustrates the government's inability to offer military aid. The idea of Britain as a distant part of the Roman world continued for at least another generation. St Germanus visited in 429 to counter an obscure theological heresy. Britain was thus thought of as part of Rome's cultural sphere. It is doubtful that any decision was ever made to cut Britain adrift, it was simply never possible to pull the western empire back together after 410.

We have insufficient historical information to provide a detailed picture of British events. The archaeological evidence is equally problematical because it changes in character. Most of the dating of Roman sites ultimately depends on historical sources or coins. In the early fifth century the historical sources are confused, while the last regular bulk supplies of bronze coin arrived in 395–402. Deposits containing coins of 395–402 are thus difficult to interpret in the absence of later datable objects. Henceforth excavated sites are only imprecisely dated.

Decline in Romanized sites began in the fourth century. Public buildings in the public towns were in poor repair and gradually went out of use. Not all Roman-style sites were deserted, and a number of fragments of major Roman buildings did survive to be incorporated into later structures. Indeed a few buildings continued to be constructed into the fifth century. There were also elaborate new timber buildings as at Wroxeter where a large house was built on top of the public baths. This was exceptional and by the end of the fourth century the defences of most public towns surrounded only a small number of functioning buildings. Towns perhaps remained centres of political authority but no longer had the urban attributes which characterized their heyday. Similarly the countryside saw a decline in the number of villas occupied and at very few was there new building in Roman style.

Major changes affected the economy. A fundamental change in demand for money occurred after 402. During earlier periods of coin shortage local imitations had been produced but this did not happen and supplies dried up. It is unlikely that the interruption of supply was seen at first as anything other than a temporary difficulty and sufficient stocks were presumably available to meet short-term needs. The subsequent failure to resume either coin supply or alternative minting, however, suggests a major change. Although this need not have signified an economic disaster there are signs of more widespread economic disruption.

One major change around the end of the fourth century was an abrupt cessation of both mass production and distribution of pottery. This was followed by a rapid end to the production of Roman-style consumer goods. This suggests a general economic collapse that coincided with the end of coin supply. Its speed is impossible to gauge given the imprecision of our dating but it appears to have happened within the first decade of the fifth century.

Different explanations have been offered to account for the loss of Britain; some emphasize external factors, others concentrate on internal matters. The external events were the barbarian depredations of the west that were experienced in Britain through attacks in 396–8 and by assaults from Saxons in 408–9. Indirectly attacks weakened Rome's ability and resolve to hold on to the province.

Explanations founded on events within Britain are varied, some seeing decline as the result of invasions, others seeing internal discontent culminating in a taxpayers' revolt. The sixth-century Greek historian Zosimus reports a revolt in 408–9 and says that the Britons expelled their Roman governors and established their own administration. Such a *coup d'état* by the nobility would explain the end of coin usage, as it was primarily associated with the rejected tax system. The revolt of 408–9 was not the sole reason for the end of the Roman system in Britain, but it perhaps provided a crucial twist in a downward spiral.

Given the few reliable sources it is only possible to outline events in Britain after 408–9. There was some continuation of Roman institutions, for instance in northwest England St Patrick's father used the titles of a Roman municipal magistrate around the year 415. The administration appears to have fragmented, with each region looking after itself, sometimes under the control of a powerful leader rather than a Roman style of council. When under military threat districts acted individually, and some followed the habit of employing barbarians to help with defence in exchange for lands on which to settle. Some of these settlers subsequently revolted and took additional lands for themselves and brought others from their homelands. The result was a piecemeal loss of territory to Germanic settlers. Elsewhere rule by Romanized leaders continued much longer despite the loss of lands in the south and east to Germanic peoples through the first half of the fifth century.

The events of the later fifth and early sixth centuries are narrated by Gildas who lived in northern Britain and wrote in the mid-sixth century. His closeness to the events is an advantage, but the value of his account is undermined, as it was a religious tract written to illustrate how episodes affecting Britain were a divine punishment. He tells of stability from 450 to about 480 following a successful war against the Saxons. Assaults were renewed in the 480s and met by a collective response from the Britons who appointed an overall commander. The final period of warfare he reports came in 495–500 when the Saxons were contained and a great British victory won at Mons Badonicus. The status quo then lasted down to the middle of the sixth century, with the sub-Roman Britons controlling lands in the west and north (see **64**), and the Saxons establishing their new cultural dominance in the south and east.

There is a little archaeological evidence for continued contact between parts of Britain and the Roman world during this period. Roman pottery from the Mediterranean entered limited areas of sub-Roman Britain in the period 475–550. It was confined to parts of the West Country about which our literary sources are silent so we can only guess at the circumstances of its arrival.

Territory in Britain passed into Germanic hands in a very different manner from that seen on the Continent. There control often passed to Romanized barbarians who were frequently Christian and adopted Roman administrative and legal systems. In Britain land was lost to pagan Saxons who brought their own religions and traditions. It was defended against these incomers over a long period by people who had already rejected aspects of *Romanitas*. Roman institutions were thus all but entirely lost and a new ascendancy established. Hence at the beginning of the Middle Ages the British Isles showed a gradation from the Germanic and pagan in the southeast, through sub-Roman Christians in Wales, the west and north of England, to the Celtic peoples of Ireland and Scotland who subsequently developed their own links with Mediterranean Christianity. These changes in political power should not obscure the fact that the majority of those who tilled the field were the heirs of the population who inhabited Iron Age Britain and the Roman province.

RETROSPECT

We have looked at what archaeology and history tell us about a short period in Britain's history when for the first time the greater part of these islands became part of a world dominated by Mediterranean culture. Readers will now appreciate that this was a period when contact with the outside world stimulated change although indigenous characteristics continued to mould society. Rich archaeological evidence shows how the lives of people changed although it also demonstrates that some were more directly influenced than others.

In the areas included within the Roman province there were evident social and economic changes. Some were the direct result of the Roman presence, but more resulted from the economic, social and administrative changes which were consequences of the new power structure. Society gradually became less dominated by tribal divisions and this coincided with the development of the idea of *Britannia* as a single, unified place. The breakdown of regional partitions was accompanied by increasing social and economic differentiation as wealth and power became concentrated in the hands of a small social group. These people became part of a culture that 'networked' them with their equals elsewhere in the empire, while the ordinary people increasingly became their dependants. Around the margins military installations first brought a new population who removed political power from the natives. As the army settled they became a naturalized but highly Romanized frontier people whose character reflected a different mixture of Roman and native characteristics. Beyond the frontiers most people remained largely unaffected by Rome except during their periodic military assaults. These areas were, however, undergoing their own evolutions towards larger scales of organization. Diplomatic contacts with the Roman government played a role in changing their internal organization, and the border peoples were increasingly attracted to migrate into Roman territory. The different patterns of social change within Britain thus culminated in the problems of the early fifth century.

In exploring this period I hope the reader will have come to appreciate something of how archaeologists work and the ways in which societies have used art, architecture and culture to create and recreate their worlds. Objects and buildings form the world in which people live and are important in defining relationships between individuals and groups. They were used by the population to proclaim themselves as Romans, and later as Germanic people. It is clear from a study of this period that all aspects of life played a part in the language through which people communicated their aspirations and achievements. Because the material from the Roman period is so rich and varied it provides a resource for understanding the past that is only paralleled from the sixteenth century in Britain. I hope that by examining this information readers will have come to a clearer appreciation of the material symbols of power that dominate our own world.

PLACES TO VISIT

Much from Roman Britain survives for the interested person to visit although the remains are not always spectacular. The best general guide is provided by R.J.A. Wilson: *A Guide to the Roman Remains in Britain* (3rd edn 1988).

MUSEUMS
There are Roman remains in most local museums but some of the best collections will be found in the following:

The National Museum of Wales, Cardiff
The Grosvenor Museum, Chester, Cheshire
The Corinium Museum, Cirencester, Gloucestershire
The Castle Museum, Colchester, Essex
The Royal Scottish Museum, Edinburgh
Transport and Archaeology Museum, Hull, East Yorkshire
Jewry Wall Museum, Leicester, Leicestershire
Lincoln City and County Museum, Lincoln, Lincolnshire
The British Museum, London
The Museum of London, London
The Museum of Antiquities, Newcastle upon Tyne, Tyne and Wear
Reading Museum and Art Gallery (Silchester collection), Reading, Berkshire
The Verulamium Museum, St Albans, Hertfordshire
The Yorkshire Museum, York, N. Yorkshire

SITES
The following Roman towns have visible remains:

Bath (with spectacular remains of the religious sanctuary)
Caerwent, Gwent
Silchester, Hampshire
Wroxeter, Shropshire

Excavated remains of villas that are well worth a visit are:

Bignor, West Sussex
Chedworth, Gloucestershire
Fishbourne, West Sussex
Littlecote, Wiltshire
Lullingstone, Kent
Rockborne, Hampshire

Most of the Saxon Shore forts are also sufficiently well preserved to be visible although the most appealing are:

Portchester, Hampshire
Richborough, Kent

The earthworks of the invasion-period fort on Hod Hill (Dorset) are worth the climb if you are energetic. Other military remains are clustered in Wales, the north of England and Scotland. Many survive as earthworks that are of interest only to the enthusiast. The most spectacular site is undoubtedly the fort at Hardknott (Cumbria).

Hadrian's Wall is best seen in its central stretch to the northwest of Hexham. The most comprehensible forts in this area are Housesteads and Chesters. However, recent work has made both South Shields in the east and Birdoswald in the west excellent alternatives that are much less crowded. At the fort and *vicus* of Vindolanda a fascinating collection of well-preserved objects is displayed in the site museum. The Antonine Wall survives only as an earthwork, which is generally not very spectacular. Few of the forts are visible although there are remains worth visiting at Bearsden on the outskirts of Glasgow and Cramond to the west of Edinburgh.

FURTHER READING

Roman Britain is a subject well provided with books. Unfortunately it is not always easy for non-specialists to judge which are the best as many repeat the same old ideas very uncritically. The following is intended as a guide to the works, which should enable the reader to find reliable books in which to read more about the ideas introduced here.

GENERAL WORKS

The standard book about Iron Age Britain is B.W. Cunliffe *Iron Age Communities in Britain* (3rd edn 1991) while S.T. James *Exploring the World of the Celts* (1993) provides an excellent general introduction. For the areas outside England the relevant chapters in J. Hunter and I. Ralston *The Archaeology of Britain: an introduction from the upper palaeolithic to the industrial revolution* (1999) is key.

The most common approach to Roman Britain has been the compilation of a traditional history using the historical texts and archaeological sources. Of the books following this approach the best is undoubtedly S.S. Frere *Britannia: a history of Roman Britain* (3rd edn 1987) although P. Salway *Roman Britain* (1981) is also useful. Of the more general works I would recommend T.W. Potter and C. Johns *Roman Britain* (1992). An alternative approach based on the archaeological evidence is my own *Romanization of Britain* (1990). A more radical approach will be found in Richard Reece *My Roman Britain* (1990).

For those wishing for a guide to the literary sources I would recommend J.C. Mann and R.G. Penman *Literary Sources for Roman Britain* (1978) although S. Ireland *Roman Britain: a sourcebook* (1986) provides further translations of relevant texts. A.R. Birley *The People of Roman Britain* (1979) uses the literary sources and inscriptions to explore aspects of the history of the province. The newly discovered Vindolanda tablets are brilliantly used to explore life on the frontier in A.K. Bowman *Life and Letters on the Roman Frontier* (2nd edn 2003).

L. Keppie *Understanding Roman Inscriptions* (1991) gives a clear introduction to Roman administration as well as the inscriptions. Life in the province is also well illustrated in L. Allason-Jones *Women in Roman Britain* (1989).

REFERENCE

In addition to these commentaries a series of books provides fundamental sources of evidence. The inscriptions are being published in the series *Roman Inscriptions of Britain* (abbreviated as R.I.B.) edited by R.G. Collingwood and R.P. Wright. Volume 1 was published in 1965 (2nd edn 1995), Volume 2 fascicules 1–8 were published 1990–95. The careers of the people involved in the province are catalogued in A.R. Birley *The Fasti of Roman Britain* (1981). The sculpture is being published in the fascicules of the *Corpus Signorum Imperii Romani* (abbreviated as C.S.I.R.), which have been appearing since 1977. The first of four volumes of the corpus *Roman Mosaics of Britain* was published in 2002 and the others will appear soon.

The topography of the province can be approached through the Ordnance Survey *Historical Map and Guide to Roman Britain* (2001) (although the *Map of Roman Britain* 1978 edition remains the best for reference). More detail can be found in G.D.B. Jones and D. Mattingly *An Atlas of Roman Britain* (1990), while the A.L.F. Rivet and C. Smith *The Place-names of Roman Britain* (1979) provides fascinating insights into a whole variety of issues.

BOOKS ON PARTICULAR THEMES

The urban sites in Britain are presented in two books, J.S. Wacher *The Towns of Roman Britain* (2nd edn 1995) and B. Burnham and J.S. Wacher *The Small Towns of Roman Britain* (1990). Villa sites are discussed in A.L.F. Rivet *The Roman Villa in Britain* (1969), M. Todd *Studies in the Romano-British Villa* (1978) and most recently in K. Branigan and D. Miles *The Economies of Romano-British Villas* (1988). A more original approach to rural sites can be found in R. Hingley *Rural Settlement in Roman Britain* (1989). The best books on the frontiers are W.S. Hanson and G. Maxwell *Rome's North-West Frontier* (1983), D. Breeze and B. Dobson *Hadrian's Wall* (4th edn 2000) and V.A. Maxwell *The Saxon Shore* (1989). S. Esmonde-Cleary *The Ending of Roman Britain* (1989) provides a lucid discussion of the later Roman provinces.

The arts and religion are less commonly discussed than other aspects of the province. A sound introduction to the Iron Age background is provided by R. Megaw and V. Megaw *Celtic Art* (1989). J.M.C. Toynbee's two books *Art in Roman Britain* (1962) and *Art in Britain under the Romans* (1964) remain fundamental, but M. Henig *Art of Roman Britain* (1995) provides an excellent new study. The books on religion take widely divergent views. M. Henig *Religion in Roman Britain* (1984) is founded in the Classical tradition. A. Ross *Pagan Celtic Britain* (1967) provides a useful survey of the Celtic material and of M. Green's several books *The Gods of the Celts* (1986) is perhaps the best. Religious sites are usefully discussed in A. Woodward *Shrines and Sacrifice* (1992). The most extensive treatment of Christianity is provided in C. Thomas *Christianity in Roman Britain to AD 500* (1981) with additional ideas presented in D. Watts *Christians and Pagans in Roman Britain* (1991). Burial evidence has been summarized in R. Philpott *Burial Practices in Roman Britain* (1991). For an introduction to coinage see Richard Reece *The Coinage of Roman Britain* (2002).

There is no full regional survey available, although the series 'The Peoples of Roman Britain' (published by Alan Sutton) covers much of the country. Although the books are very variable in quality and now rather outdated, they still provide a useful starting point for further reading. The volumes available to date are: B. Cunliffe *The Regni* (1973), M. Todd *The Coritani* (2nd edn 1991), R. Dunnett *The Trinovantes* (1975), G. Webster *The Cornovii* (2nd edn 1991), H. Ramm *The Parisi* (1978), A.P. Detsicas *The Cantiaci* (1983), K. Branigan *The Catuvellauni* (1985), N. Higham and G.D.B. Jones *The Carvetii* (1985) and B.R. Hartley and L. Fitz *The Brigantes* (1988).

FURTHER INFORMATION

Research on Roman Britain is undertaken by a wide range of organizations. Annual reviews of work undertaken are published by the Society for the Promotion of Roman Studies in their journal *Britannia*. They also arrange lectures and publish occasional books on Roman subjects. More popular accounts of fieldwork are published in the magazines *Current Archaeology* and *British Archaeology*. For further information on archaeology in Britain contact should be made with *The Council for British Archaeology*.

GLOSSARY

ambulatory Roofed walkway around the central shrine, or cella, of a Romano-Celtic temple.

auxiliary Soldier in a Roman army unit originally recruited from among conquered peoples. The *auxilia* generally comprised units of about 500 men, used for tactical purposes, who sometimes had specialist fighting skills.

baptistry Small building, separate from the church, which housed the baptismal font in early Christian churches.

basilica Type of rectangular building in which the central area (nave) has a single-span pitched roof along its axis, with the two subsidiary spaces on either side (the aisles) covered by lean-to roofs. Such buildings could hold large numbers of people so were used for the principal public buildings in towns. The building type thus gives its name to the principal administrative building of the town, located alongside the forum. The form was widely adopted for use in church building.

cella Central shrine of a temple.

Celtic Term widely used to describe both the peoples of central and western Europe during the Iron Age and the abstract symmetrical art style of the period. In modern times it has come to be used to describe the various peoples who speak languages akin to Welsh.

censor One of a pair of senior magistrates at Rome, a post usually held by those who had already been consuls.

chi-rho First and second letters of the name of Christ in Greek. They were used as a symbol in early Christianity (see **78**).

civitas (pl. *civitates*) The basic unit of Roman government as applied to Roman Britain. Indigenous tribes became *civitates* and were treated as though they were *city* states. Thus their territory was governed by a council drawn from the local landowners who used a central town (the *civitas*-capital) as their centre of government.

classis Britannica The Roman naval fleet that patrolled the English Channel.

coloni Peasant labourers of the late empire who were required by law to remain on their landlord's property.

colonia (pl. *coloniae*) A town founded by Rome to house those who held Roman citizenship. In Britain this usually meant those who had completed their service in the Roman legions and were thus owed a grant of land by the State.

comes Literally a companion; becomes, count, a military leader in the later empire who commanded a mobile field-army unit.

comitatenses The mobile field army of the later empire.

consul One of the pair of chief magistrates elected by the Roman Senate.

cremation The ash from a burnt human body.

currency bar Long iron bar, or ingot, used in the Iron Age.

defixio (pl. *defixiones*) Small tablet (strictly one that is nailed to something), usually of lead, with a curse or message to the gods inscribed upon it.

dendrochronology Method of establishing the age of timbers by comparing the patterns of their growth rings with those from trees of known date.

diocese A later Roman administrative unit that comprised a series of adjacent provinces.

emperor The man who was military commander-in-chief, chief priest and held delegated powers from the Senate, who had effective power within the Roman system of government. In theory his power derived from the Senate although in practice it relied on control of the army.

equestrian An ill-defined social rank within Roman society intermediate between that of Senators and ordinary citizens.

font Container for baptismal water. In the early Christian church it was commonly large enough for an adult to stand in.

forum The focal public square at the centre of a Roman town, which acted as the main meeting-place. In Britain it was usually surrounded on three sides by shops and on the fourth by a basilica.

Gaul Roman name for the area now covered by France, Belgium and parts of the Low Countries.

governor The emperor's personal representative in a province who commanded the army, had judicial power and watched over the government of the *civitates*.

hill-fort Hilltop surrounded by one or more circuits of defences, usually earthen ramparts. Most date to the Iron Age, and some contained permanently occupied settlements. Others were refuges or centres for occasional gatherings.

hoard Group of objects that has been amassed and hidden, often in the ground.

imperator Latin term for the military commander-in-chief.

inhumation A burial in which the body is laid out in the grave unburnt.

interpretatio Romana Literally 'the Roman interpretation'. A term used in connection with the Roman practice of identifying individual native gods with particular gods of their own.

Iron Age Period of prehistory during which iron came into use. The term pre-Roman Iron Age is generally used to refer to the period from c. 800–600 BC down to the Roman invasion. In areas outside the empire the term Roman Iron Age is used for the period of the first–fourth centuries AD.

lanx Silver platter or large dish.

legion (Latin *legio)* Military unit recruited from among Roman citizens and generally used for strategic purposes during the imperial period. Each legion was just over 5000 men in strength.

limitanei Later Roman frontier troops from units who were permanently stationed in forts around the borders of the empire.

luminescence dating Method of establishing the date at which a mineral was last heated by measuring the light given off when it is reheated or stimulated with a laser. It is based on the principle that some crystals, which collect radiation from their surroundings, release it again, giving off light, when they are heated.

magistrate An official annually elected by the Senate to undertake administrative duties. In Roman practice each shared power with at least one equal colleague. This system was also widely adopted for the administration of the towns in the provinces.

mansio (pl. *mansiones)* An inn provided for official travellers on the principal roads through the empire.

martyrium (pl. **martyria)** Burial place of a Christian martyr that later became a place of worship.

mausoleum (pl. **mausolea)** Small building in a cemetery within which people were buried.

Mithraeum (pl. **Mithraea)** A temple to the Oriental god Mithras.

municipium (pl. *municipia)* An existing town rewarded by Rome with special rights of citizenship.

mutatio (pl. *mutationes)* A way-station provided for official travellers on the principal roads through the empire.

oppidum (pl. *oppida)* A generic term in Latin loosely meaning town. It is widely used by archaeologists to denote the large lowland sites defined by earthworks and natural features that were a characteristic of the late pre-Roman Iron Age.

procurator Official drawn from the equestrian class who had responsibilities for financial matters. The procurator of a province was its chief financial officer.

province Territorial administrative unit within the Roman empire under the control of a governor.

public town Generic term used to describe those Roman towns (*civitates, coloniae* and *municipia*) that functioned as the principal administrative centres for their districts and thus had an array of public buildings.

radiocarbon dating Method of establishing the age of a sample of organic material by measuring the ratio of the two isotopes of carbon (^{14}C to ^{12}C) within the sample. It is based on the fact that the ^{14}C in living organisms decays to ^{12}C after their death at a known rate.

rath Term used in Wales and Ireland to describe a roughly circular farmstead surrounded by an earthwork bank.

Roman citizenship Legally, membership of the citizen body of the city of Rome. Roman citizenship was given to provincials as a reward for service and loyalty.

Romanized Term used to describe the acquisition by native peoples of cultural characteristics associated with Rome. These included both the use of Roman-style goods and the adoption of Roman manners including the Latin language.

Romano-Celtic temple Type of temple common in Britain and across Gaul in which the central shrine (usually square in plan) is surrounded by a concentric ambulatory.

round Term used in Cornwall to describe a roughly circular farmstead surrounded by an earthwork bank.

Senate The legally supreme constitutional authority of the Roman State made up from an assembly of 600 men qualified for service by their wealth and family status.

small town A nucleated settlement with urban characteristics that did not function as the administrative centre for a district.

temenos The sacred area enclosed within the precinct surrounding a temple.

torc Neck-ring, often of gold or other precious metal, worn both during the Iron Age and also as a military decoration in the Roman army.

tree-ring dating see **dendrochronology.**

tribune A man granted powers by the Senate that gave him authority over them and the magistrates.

vallum The ditch, with a bank set back on either side, which stood to the south of Hadrian's Wall, probably to define the military zone behind it.

vicarius Later Roman administrative official in charge of a diocese.

vicus (pl. ***vici***) This term has two separate meanings. In legal terms it referred to the administrative centre of a subdivision of a *civitas*. In archaeological usage it refers to the dependent settlement that stood outside a Roman fort.

villa Romanized house in the countryside used by landowners to display their wealth and status.

Visigothic Western Gothic or Germanic tribes who invaded Italy and sacked Rome in AD 410.

votive Something which has been offered in fulfilment of a religious vow.

INDEX

(Numbers in **bold** refer to illustrations)

Aaron, martyr 114
administrative systems 7, 18, 45–54,
  68–72, 130, 133
Agricola, governor **6**, 6, **8**, 9, 15, 31, 33
agriculture 23–24, 38–40, 58, 66–7, 77
Allectus, usurper 12
Alton **100**
Ammianus Marcellinus 12, 15
Anglesey 8, 104
Antonine, Itinerary 15
  Wall **8**, 10
Antoninus Pius, emperor **8**, 10, **14**
Aquileia **63**
archaeological evidence 16–22
army 23, 31–2, 37, 54–5, **61**, **63**, 72–6,
  88, **89**, 92–3, 97–9, 104, **105**, 131
art 46, 85–99
Ashton **101**
Atrebates, *civitas* **17**, **42**
Augustus, emperor 8
Aurelian, emperor 12
Aurelius Victor 12

Bagshot **94**
Bartlow Hills **98**, **99**
Bath 74, **75**, **90**, 91–2, 108, 112, 114
Belgae, *civitas* **42**
Bigberry, slave chain **24**
Binchester **71**
Birdlip **68**
Birdoswold **64**
Boudicca 8, **41**, **44**, 46, 52
Boulogne 81
Braughing 28
Bridgeness **86**
Brigantes, *civitas* and tribe **4**, 8, 10, **32**,
  42, 47, 110
Brough-on-Humber **40**
Burgh Castle **61**
burials 21, **37**, 88, **98**, **99**, 100, **100**, **101**,
  102, **103**, 116–7, 119–29
Butser, ancient farmstead **19**

Caerleon **7**, 114
Caesar, Julius 5, 6, 8, 15
Caledonians, tribe 12, **31**, **32**, 34
Calleva, *see* Silchester
Camerton **58**
Camulodunon (Camulodunum) **4**, **5**, 8,
  17, **18**, **22**, 28, **43**, 48, 49, 52,
  105–6, 122
Canterbury (Durovernon) **17**, **95**
Cantiaci, *civitas* **17**, **42**
Cantii, *see* Cantiaci
Caracalla, emperor 12
Carausius, usurper 12
Carlisle 18, 20, 32, **77**
Carpow, fort **9**
Carvetii, *civitas* **32**, **42**
Catuvellauni, *civitas* and tribe 8, **17**, 28,
  42, 48, 50
cemeteries, *see* burials
Charterhouse 60
Chester **6**, **7**, 32
Christianity 34, **78**, **80**, **94**, **95**, **96**, **97**,
  103, 104, 113–19, 126, 128, 129,
  134
churches **95**, **96**, 115–17
Cirencester 58, 70, **79**, **95**, 125
citizenship 45, 49, 50, 52, 71
civitas organization 25, 28, 47–8, 49, 53,
  68, 71, 78, 80, 82, 83
Classicianus, *procurator* 41
classis Britannica 81
Claudian 14
Claudius, emperor **2**, **3**, 6, 8, 28, **43**, 48,
  71, 105
Clodius Albinus, governor and usurper
  11, 57, 70
Cogidubnus, king **4**, 46, 62, 71, 91
coins **14**, **18**, 18, 25, 28, 48, 55, 70, 77,
  79, 101, 102, 126, 132, 133
Colchester, *see* Camulodunon
Collingwood, R.G. 89
coloni 66

comes 73
comitatenses 73
Commodus, emperor 11
Constans, emperor 12
Constantine, Cornwall, round **26**
Constantine I, emperor 12, 115, 128
Constantine III, emperor 14, 131
Constantius, emperor 12
copper mining 81
Corbridge **9**, 32, **66**
Corieltauvi, *civitas* **17**, **42**
Cornovii, *civitas* 12, **42**
Coventina's well 112
Cowdery's Down **102**
Cunobelinus 18
cursus publicus 53

defixiones **90**, 109, 114
Degeangli, *civitas* **42**
Demetae, *civitas* **42**
dendrochronology 15, **20**, 20
Derbyshire, mines 40, 80
Dio Cassius 8, 11, 12
Diocletian, emperor 12
Ditchley **52**
Dobunni, *civitas* **17**, **42**
Dolaucothi 81
Dorchester, Dorset **104**, 126, 129
Dover 81
Droitwich 60
druids 8, 104–5
Dumnonii, *civitas* **42**
Dunstable 128
Dunovernum, *see* Canterbury
Durotriges, *civitas* **17**, 27, **42**

Eastgate, Co. Durham **87**
Eildon Hill, 33
emperor, office of 68
Eutropius 12
Exuperius, bishop **80**, 117